The present report was prepared by the MDG Gap Task Force, which was created by the Secretary-General of the United Nations to improve the monitoring of MDG 8 by leveraging inter-agency coordination. More than 30 United Nations entities and other organizations are represented in the Task Force, including the World Bank and the International Monetary Fund, as well as the Organization for Economic Cooperation and Development and the World Trade Organization. The Department of Economic and Social Affairs of the United Nations Secretariat (UN/DESA) and the United Nations Development Programme (UNDP) acted as lead agencies in organizing the work of the Task Force. The coordination was performed by Pingfan Hong, Director, and Keiji Inoue, Economic Affairs Officer, in the Development Policy and Analysis Division of UN/DESA.

List of bodies and agencies represented on the MDG Gap Task Force

---

Department of Economic and Social Affairs of the United Nations Secretariat (UN/DESA)

Department of Public Information of the United Nations Secretariat (DPI)

Economic and Social Commission for Asia and the Pacific (ESCAP)

Economic and Social Commission for Western Asia (ESCWA)

Economic Commission for Africa (ECA)

Economic Commission for Europe (ECE)

Economic Commission for Latin America and the Caribbean (ECLAC)

International Labour Organization (ILO)

International Monetary Fund (IMF)

International Telecommunication Union (ITU)

International Trade Centre (ITC)

Joint United Nations Programme on HIV/AIDS (UNAIDS)

Office of the United Nations High Commissioner for Human Rights (OHCHR)

Organization for Economic Cooperation and Development (OECD)

United Nations Children's Fund (UNICEF)

United Nations Conference on Trade and Development (UNCTAD)

United Nations Development Programme (UNDP)

United Nations Educational, Scientific and Cultural Organization (UNESCO)

United Nations Framework Convention on Climate Change (UNFCCC)

United Nations Fund for International Partnerships (UNFIP)

United Nations Industrial Development Organization (UNIDO)

United Nations Institute for Training and Research (UNITAR)

United Nations International Strategy for Disaster Reduction (UNISDR)

United Nations Office for Project Services (UNOPS)

United Nations Office of the High Representative for the Least Developed Countries, Landlocked Developing Countries and Small Island Developing States (UN-OHRLLS)

United Nations Population Fund (UNFPA)

United Nations Research Institute for Social Development (UNRISD)

World Bank

World Food Programme (WFP)

World Health Organization (WHO)

World Institute for Development Economics Research of the United Nations University (UNU-WIDER)

World Intellectual Property Organization (WIPO)

World Meteorological Organization (WMO)

World Tourism Organization (UNWTO)

World Trade Organization (WTO)

Millennium Development Goal 8

The State
of the Global Partnership
for Development

MDG Gap Task Force Report 2014

United Nations
New York, 2014

United Nations publication
Sales No. E.14.I.7
ISBN 978-92-1-101304-7
eISBN 978-92-1-056820-3

Preface

The deadline for achieving the Millennium Development Goals (MDGs) is fast approaching, with much progress to report and many challenges still ahead. The present report serves to review the experiences of recent years in pursuing a global partnership for development. Its analysis is particularly important as the international community focuses on formulating the post-2015 development agenda.

Since 2007, the MDG Gap Task Force has examined progress and shortfalls in implementing the targets of Goal 8, to "develop a global partnership for development". Each report focuses on the gap between commitments made and cooperation delivered, with the ultimate goal of helping the international community bridge the difference.

A number of targets for Goal 8 are close to being achieved. Duty-free and quota-free access to developed-country markets has been extended for exports from least developed countries. Countries eligible for the Heavily Indebted Poor Countries Initiative have successfully completed that process and achieved substantial and irrevocable debt relief. At the same time, progress on other targets has been slow, in particular in reaching the pledged volumes of official development assistance (ODA). There are important exceptions, and I applaud those States that have continued to increase ODA.

Private investment has spurred the greater availability and falling cost of telecommunications across the developing world, but too many people continue to lack access to affordable essential medicines. We still need an effective convergence of public policies and private initiatives to bridge this gap.

Once again, the MDG Gap Task Force Report has brought together key information produced by different parts of the international system, presenting a coherent overall picture of development cooperation. The report identifies what works as well as what remains to be done to realize an effective partnership.

Now more than ever, leaders and citizens across the globe must boldly step forward to join in essential collective actions to eradicate poverty, raise living standards and sustain the environment.

I call on all Governments and international institutions to continue strengthening the global partnership for development so that we can usher in a more sustainable future.

Ban Ki-moon
Secretary-General of the United Nations

Contents

List of Millennium Development Goals and Goal 8 targets and indicators

Goals 1 to 7

Goal 1: Eradicate extreme poverty and hunger

Goal 2: Achieve universal primary education

Goal 3: Promote gender equality and empower women

Goal 4: Reduce child mortality

Goal 5: Improve maternal health

Goal 6: Combat HIV/AIDS, malaria and other diseases

Goal 7: Ensure environmental sustainability

Goal 8: Develop a global partnership for development	
Targets	Indicators

Some of the indicators listed below are monitored separately for the least developed countries (LDCs), Africa, landlocked developing countries and small island developing States.

Target 8.A: Develop further an open, rule-based, predictable, non-discriminatory trading and financial system

Includes a commitment to good governance, development and poverty reduction—both nationally and internationally

Target 8.B: Address the special needs of the least developed countries

Includes tariff and quota free access for the least developed countries' exports; enhanced programme of debt relief for heavily indebted poor countries (HIPC) and cancellation of official bilateral debt; and more generous ODA for countries committed to poverty reduction

Target 8.C: Address the special needs of landlocked developing countries and small island developing States (through the Programme of Action for the Sustainable Development of Small Island Developing States and the outcome of the twenty-second special session of the General Assembly)

Official development assistance (ODA)

8.1 Net ODA, total and to the least developed countries, as percentage of OECD/DAC donors' gross national incomes

8.2 Proportion of total bilateral, sector-allocable ODA of OECD/DAC donors to basic social services (basic education, primary health care, nutrition, safe water and sanitation)

8.3 Proportion of bilateral official development assistance of OECD/DAC donors that is untied

8.4 ODA received in landlocked developing countries as a proportion of their gross national incomes

8.5 ODA received in small island developing States as a proportion of their gross national incomes

Market access

8.6 Proportion of total developed country imports (by value and excluding arms) from developing countries and least developed countries admitted free of duty

8.7 Average tariffs imposed by developed countries on agricultural products and textiles and clothing from developing countries

8.8 Agricultural support estimate for OECD countries as a percentage of their gross domestic product

8.9 Proportion of ODA provided to help build trade capacity

Goal 8: Develop a global partnership for development *(continued)*

Targets	Indicators
	Debt sustainability
Target 8.D: Deal comprehensively with the debt problems of developing countries through national and international measures in order to make debt sustainable in the long term	**8.10** Total number of countries that have reached their HIPC decision points and number that have reached their HIPC completion points (cumulative)
	8.11 Debt relief committed under HIPC and MDRI Initiatives
	8.12 Debt service as a percentage of exports of goods and services
Target 8.E: In cooperation with pharmaceutical companies, provide access to affordable essential drugs in developing countries	**8.13** Proportion of population with access to affordable essential drugs on a sustainable basis
Target 8.F: In cooperation with the private sector, make available the benefits of new technologies, especially information and communications	**8.14** Fixed telephone lines per 100 inhabitants
	8.15 Mobile cellular subscriptions per 100 inhabitants
	8.16 Internet users per 100 inhabitants

Executive summary

The MDG Gap Task Force, an inter-agency collaboration created by the United Nations Secretary-General in 2007, is responsible for monitoring the policy commitments embodied in the Millennium Declaration and earlier international agreements, identified as the targets of Goal 8 of the Millennium Development Goals (MDGs).

As previous reports of the Task Force indicate, there have been positive developments that point to an effective international partnership, but shortfalls in development cooperation highlight the need for a revitalized global partnership for development as the international community moves towards delivering a post-2015 development agenda.

The global partnership for development

Several lessons can be drawn from monitoring Goal 8 that have implications for monitoring the global partnership for development under a new development agenda: first, there is a need to strengthen the linkages between Goal 8 and other goals; second, global monitoring of the partnership initiatives is an essential task; third, the successor to Goal 8 should periodically be reviewed for continued relevance; and fourth, efforts to attain the MDGs should not be confused with the broader, long-standing international commitment to foster sustainable development.

In preparation for the post-2015 development agenda, discussions are being held to propose a comprehensive financing framework to underpin these development efforts. In order to make this a reality, a renewed political commitment to development cooperation is imperative.

Official development assistance

Official development assistance (ODA) flows reached a record $135 billion[1] in 2013, helping to alleviate concerns about two consecutive years of falling volumes. The 2013 result represents 0.3 per cent of combined Organization for Economic Cooperation and Development (OECD) Development Assistance Committee (DAC) donors' gross national income (GNI), a marginal improvement in meeting the United Nations target of disbursing 0.7 per cent of donor GNI. Aid to least developed countries (LDCs) increased by 12.3 per cent in 2013 compared with the previous year.

A number of concerns remain, however. Aid is still heavily concentrated, with the top 20 recipients receiving 53 per cent of total ODA in 2012. Prelimi-

---

[1] All monetary amounts are expressed in United States dollars, except where otherwise indicated.

nary data show a 4 per cent decrease in bilateral aid to sub-Saharan Africa in 2013, to $26.2 billion. The aid portfolios for landlocked developing countries have stagnated since 2010, and those for small island developing States declined for a second straight year in 2012. Flows of official and private concessional development financing also fell in 2012. Finally, forward spending plans of major donors do not indicate a significant growth in ODA flows in the medium term.

Nevertheless, United Nations Member States continue to call for donors to meet the target of disbursing 0.7 per cent of GNI as ODA by 2015. Member countries of the Group of Eight reaffirmed their commitments to sustainable global food and nutrition security, and a global coalition of developed and developing countries have pledged a record $52 billion in financing over the next three years to the World Bank's International Development Association. In addition, the Global Partnership for Effective Development Cooperation committed to working with the United Nations Development Cooperation Forum to help strengthen recipient Governments' ownership over development cooperation programmes and both recipient and donor Governments' mutual accountability mechanisms.

Policy recommendations

- Donor Governments must accelerate their efforts to achieve the United Nations target of disbursing 0.7 per cent of their GNI in ODA by 2015
- Donor Governments must increase the share of ODA to priority groups of countries
- Non-DAC countries and other development actors are urged to continue to provide and scale up their development cooperation
- Member States are encouraged to build on the discussions at the Fourth High-level Meeting of the Development Cooperation Forum to develop a more inclusive, accountable and effective development cooperation

Market access

A central concern of Goal 8 has been to support developing countries to attain the MDGs through economic growth, helped by export growth, and supported by an open, rule-based, predictable and non-discriminatory trading system. Notably, developed countries have lowered tariffs considerably and their proportion of imports from developing countries admitted duty free continues to increase. Agricultural subsidies in OECD countries were little changed in 2013, but remained lower than in previous years. Donor countries and institutions have continued to support developing-country efforts to build trade capacity through initiatives such as Aid for Trade. However, despite the commitment by members of the Group of Twenty, the number of new trade restrictions increased in 2013. Tariff peaks continue to affect market access opportunities, and tariff escalations, which impact products at later stages of production, increased in 2013.

Encouragingly, a breakthrough in trade negotiations in the form of the Bali Package was achieved in late 2013. This Package included agreements on trade facilitation, agriculture, a package of decisions for the LDCs and a monitoring system on special and differential treatment (SDT) provisions. While promising, the decisions taken in Bali cover only a subset of the issues of the Doha Round, and a clearly defined programme of work to conclude the Round is yet to be completed.

Policy recommendations

- All countries should remove trade-restrictive measures adopted since the global economic crisis and avoid introducing new ones
- Developed countries should eliminate all forms of agricultural export subsidies and trade-distorting domestic support
- Developed countries should increase support for capacity-building in developing countries
- World Trade Organization (WTO) members should strive to achieve the goals of the Bali Package, particularly those on agriculture, in order to reach a balanced conclusion of the Doha Round

Debt sustainability

Debt relief under the Heavily Indebted Poor Countries (HIPC) Initiative and the Multilateral Debt Relief Initiative has alleviated debt burdens in assisted countries and has helped increase poverty-reducing expenditure. The HIPC Initiative is now drawing to a close, but several HIPC countries are once again approaching moderate or high levels of debt distress.

The external debt of the developing countries as a whole declined to 22.6 per cent of their combined gross domestic product (GDP) in 2013, down more than 10 percentage points over the past decade. However, short-term debt levels and debt servicing burdens have continued to rise, indicating a growing vulnerability in the short term while fiscal deficits have widened. Small States (as defined by the Commonwealth Secretariat) present significant debt sustainability challenges and require country-specific efforts to address them. In 2013, the average ratio of public debt to GDP of small States amounted to 107.7 per cent, compared to a ratio of 26.4 per cent for developing countries as a whole.

A number of frameworks exist to evaluate debt sustainability, such as the joint World Bank-International Monetary Fund (IMF) Debt Sustainability Framework and the IMF Debt Sustainability Analysis for Market Access Countries. However, there remains a need for an enhanced approach to debt restructurings which considers the changing composition of developing-country debt. Going forward, the international community's task is to assist developing countries in effectively managing their current levels of debt and to avoid building up unsustainable levels of debt in the future.

Policy recommendations

- International financial institutions should strengthen the methodology for debt sustainability analyses, taking account of the financing options available and the situations of developing countries
- The international community should assure timely and equitable debt relief for critically indebted developing countries
- Governments should strike a social and developmental balance while implementing adjustment policies to reduce debt burdens
- The international community should convoke an international working group to examine options for enhancing the international architecture for sovereign debt restructuring

Access to essential medicines

In order to improve access to medicines, treatments must not only be sufficiently available and appropriately priced, but must also be affordable to patients. Between 2007 and 2013, availability of generic medicines in both the public and private sectors of developing countries remained low (55 per cent and 66 per cent, respectively). Prices of generic medicines also remain high for patients in low- and lower-middle-income countries, averaging three times international reference prices. Further, there is a critical need to find policy and legislative solutions that will assure the quality of medicines.

Nevertheless, there are some efforts to increase treatment access. The WTO Trade-related Aspects of Intellectual Property Rights (TRIPS) Agreement contains certain flexibilities which allow developing countries to manage their own intellectual property systems, and pharmaceutical companies can also promote the supply of generic medicines in developing countries by entering voluntary licensing agreements. LDCs are exempt from complying with the TRIPS Agreement with respect to pharmaceutical products until 2016 and have a general extension with respect to the implementation of the TRIPS Agreement, except for non-discrimination, until 1 July 2021. This allows LDCs the opportunity to create viable technological bases and to overcome various capacity constraints, including technology transfer. Many multi-stakeholder partnerships in developing countries are also aiming to improve access to medicines.

Policy recommendations

- Countries should address the existence of spurious/falsely labelled/falsified/counterfeit medicines in order to ensure quality without impeding access to treatment
- Developing countries are encouraged to take advantage of the flexibilities offered in the TRIPS Agreement and develop policies that foster access to essential medicines
- While efforts to increase access to antiretroviral drugs in low-income countries should continue, focus should also be given to middle-income countries where AIDS is prevalent

Access to new technologies

Developing-country access to advanced technologies continues to grow at a fast pace, particularly in mobile telephony and Internet usage. By the end of 2014, penetration rates of mobile-cellular subscriptions in developing countries will reach 90 per cent, compared with 121 per cent in developed countries. Similarly, growth in Internet usage in developing countries continues to outpace that in developed countries. Further, by the end of 2014, 711 million people in the world are expected to have fixed-broadband subscriptions—twice as many as in 2009.

Yet, despite these gains, gaps in access to advanced technologies still persist between developed and developing countries. While mobile-broadband penetration is expected to reach 84 per cent in 2014 in developed countries, it is estimated to barely exceed 21 per cent in developing countries. A similar gap exists in fixed-broadband penetration rates between developed and developing countries (28 per cent and 6 per cent, respectively).

Several international initiatives to augment access to and use of information and communication technologies (ICT) have been launched. There are also a number of efforts to conceptualize a new ICT monitoring framework that includes setting appropriate targets, indicators and strong linkages to a broader development agenda. Further, the use of advanced technology to respond to developing countries' needs for access to technologies that address the impact of climate change and for use in disaster risk reduction efforts is growing in importance. Governments are increasingly using ICT and e-government approaches to promote and to achieve development agendas. National and local governments have been collaboratively using e-government to simplify administrative procedures and to provide information to their citizens.

Policy recommendations

- Governments of developing countries, in cooperation with the private sector, should make efforts to provide more affordable broadband Internet services through an open and fair regulatory system
- Considering the impact and potential of broadband networks, services and applications on the achievement of the MDGs, all countries are encouraged to provide broadband Internet to all citizens
- Governments should support the development of policies for innovation, while enabling faster diffusion of technologies to support sustainable development
- Countries with the expertise should continue to share information regarding more effective tools for disaster risk reduction, including asset and risk assessment

Towards a new global partnership for development

This is the seventh in a series of reports on the global partnership for development prepared by the MDG Gap Task Force, an inter-agency collaboration created in 2007 by the United Nations Secretary-General. In each report, the Task Force has sought to monitor the state of implementation of those policy commitments embodied in the Millennium Declaration, and earlier international agreements, that were collected together and identified as the targets of Goal 8—develop a global partnership for development—of the Millennium Development Goals (MDGs). While many developments in the areas monitored by the Task Force point to an effective international partnership, there have also been disappointing shortfalls to which the Task Force has drawn attention. Over time, the Task Force became increasingly concerned about the disappointments, a concern reflected in the subtitles of its reports:

2008: *Delivering on the Global Partnership for achieving the Millennium Development Goals*

2009: *Strengthening the Global Partnership for Development in a Time of Crisis*

2010: *The Global Partnership for Development at a Critical Juncture*

2011: *The Global Partnership for Development: Time to Deliver*

2012: *The Global Partnership for Development: Making Rhetoric a Reality*

2013: *The Global Partnership for Development: The Challenge We Face*

As the following chapters demonstrate, certain modest progress has been realized during 2013 that hints at a recovery, albeit tentative, after a lapse in the momentum in global development cooperation during the two previous years. Of particular importance is the 2013 rebound in the aggregate volume of official development assistance (ODA) (although aid for Africa fell). Also, at the Ministerial Meeting of the World Trade Organization (WTO) in Bali in December 2013, countries agreed to undertake a modest agenda of new trade-enhancing measures for the benefit of developing countries, even though negotiations towards the primary aspirations of the WTO 2001 Doha Development Agenda remain largely unfinished. The gap between the Goal 8 targets and policy delivery thus remains wide.

There is no reason to conclude from the shortfalls in development cooperation that Governments reconsidered the aspirations embraced by Goal 8 or that the inherent capability of the partners to deliver on their commitments was compromised. Rather, the weak trend detailed in the series of reports of the MDG Gap Task Force seems to reflect a conflict between national priorities to deliver on the commitments of Goal 8 and national policy obligations sometimes derived from economic and social difficulties. This poses a special challenge to the United Nations community as it embarks on a set of negotiations that will lead to a renewed global partnership to deliver a post-2015 development agenda.[1] As part of those deliberations, the international community will need to revitalize the political commitment that had accompanied the global partnership in the early years of the new millennium as well as update the intrinsic content of the partnership.

Lessons from monitoring Goal 8 targets and indicators

As may be seen in the full statement of the targets and indicators of Goal 8 that are reproduced at the beginning of the present report, Goal 8 asked the Governments of developed countries to extend specific types of support to developing countries in the service of helping them to realize Goals 1 through 7. It could reasonably have been expected that were the targets of Goal 8 reached, developing countries would have strengthened their earnings from trade and eased their sovereign debt difficulties so that, coupled with enhanced ODA and appropriate access to new technologies, including those embodied in essential medicines, each country would be in a better position to attain the goals. But the package of policy targets in Goal 8 had not been explicitly conceived and discussed as a unified, comprehensive set of policies to deliver the MDGs. The targets, which were first specified in the 2001 report of the Secretary-General on a road map towards the implementation of the United Nations Millennium Declaration (A/56/326), had been extracted from selected statements in the Millennium Declaration and various earlier international agreements. As a result, Goal 8 has been frequently criticized for lacking precision, coherence or direct links to the other MDGs.[2]

Deepening monitoring and advocacy

In fact, the Secretary-General created the present inter-agency Task Force in 2007 in recognition that additional analytical work was required to supplement the targets and indicators of Goal 8. For example, while target 8.D called upon the international community to deal comprehensively with the sovereign debt problems of developing countries to make their debt "sustainable" in the long term, no debt sustainability indicator had been specified, whereas considerable work has since been undertaken on debt sustainability at the Bretton Woods institutions and elsewhere (as now reflected in the Task Force reports). Similarly, while target 8.E called for access to "affordable" essential medicines in developing countries, the associated indicator did not specify how to measure affordability; the Task Force thus introduced various indicators, including the World Health Organization estimates of the number of days of wages the lowest-paid unskilled government worker would need to purchase a 30-day supply of a particular medicine.

Moreover, Governments were making additional commitments that related to what Goal 8 was meant to encompass. Thus, the Task Force not only deepened the monitoring of the targets and indicators that had originally been specified, but it monitored implementation of related additional commitments, such as the

---

1 United Nations General Assembly resolution 68/6.
2 See United Nations System Task Team on the Post-2015 Development Agenda, "Assessment of MDG8 and lessons learnt: thematic think piece," January 2013, New York.

donor ODA volume commitments targeted for achievement by 2010 that had been made at the Gleneagles Summit of the Group of Eight (G8) in 2005, and the aid-effectiveness targets adopted in 2005 and 2008, also for achievement by 2010.[3]

Furthermore, the Secretary-General implicitly added to the scope of Goal 8 when, beginning in 2010, he undertook a number of initiatives to focus the attention of public policymakers and private actors around the world on mobilizing additional resources for and actions on selected MDGs. The initiatives include Every Woman Every Child, Sustainable Energy for All, the Global Education First Initiative, Zero Hunger Challenge, the Scaling Up Nutrition Movement, and the Call to Action on Sanitation. These initiatives are highly focused collections of voluntary partnerships involving Governments, multilateral and regional institutions, foundations, civil society organizations and for-profit enterprises, serving to encourage multi-stakeholder collaboration on individual projects and programmes—by publicizing announced arrangements, for example. The United Nations has also publicized a large number of MDG-related partnerships that do not fall within the initiatives of the Secretary-General, many of which are announced at high-level meetings at the United Nations and elsewhere.[4] In all, these initiatives reflect the growing set of development cooperation partners and actors and the growing recognition in development policy circles of the potential participation of the for-profit sector in development partnerships.[5]

Together, these partnership arrangements and initiatives will surely advance the world towards attaining the MDGs, but they do not guarantee full delivery of the goals by the 2015 target. First, announced projects are voluntary arrangements and in some cases entail aspirational or contingent commitments. Second, they are specific arrangements in specific countries for specific purposes and as such will not necessarily improve conditions across the board in a comprehensive manner. Partnerships are a valuable but "bottom-up" approach and require a large complement of "top-down" inputs by the international community to fill in the gaps.

Implications of the monitoring experience

In all, some implications for future monitoring of the global partnership for development can be found in the MDG experience. First, if Goal 8 is meant to undergird the global efforts to achieve the MDGs, then the association between the renewed global partnership for development and the rest of the goals should be significantly strengthened. This does not mean that it is necessary or even appropriate to associate means of implementation with each separate goal. Clearly, spreading the availability of potable water and basic sanitation (target 7.C) will contribute to reducing the mortality rate of children under age five (target 4.A). But some effort to link global partnership actions to individual or clustered goals

---

3   For these and other additions to the originally mandated indicators, see *MDG Gap Task Force Report 2013: The Global Partnership for Development—The Challenge We Face* (United Nations publication, Sales No. E.13.I.5), box 1.

4   These initiatives are tracked on the website of the Integrated Implementation Framework, available from iif.un.org.

5   Although targets 8.E on essential medicines and 8.F on technology made explicit reference to cooperation with the private sector, no indicators were specified to monitor that cooperation and none have yet been introduced in the Task Force reports.

seems warranted, if for no other reason than the fact that particular social or environmental factors often motivate greater participation by contributing actors.

Second, global monitoring of the many partnership initiatives to advance towards the goals is an essential task. It is, however, a difficult challenge, not only because the reporting of announced partnerships is spotty and follow-up information may not be available to the general public, but also because very many of the initiatives are unreported, especially those carried out by thousands of domestic and international civil society organizations. Such a decentralized system of cooperation as now exists may not be sufficient to achieve each of the goals in each country. Global oversight should therefore seek to identify the gaps and advocate concrete steps to address them.

Third, with a target end point that was 15 years from the initiation of the MDGs, it would be (and was) unlikely that the specific targets and indicators of Goal 8 would remain as saliently meaningful more than a decade later. It has already been mentioned that additional ODA targets were adopted by the G8 in 2005, which the Task Force monitored until their expiry in 2010. It could also be noted that the sovereign debt target under Goal 8 was monitored through three indicators, two of which pertained to the Heavily Indebted Poor Countries (HIPC) Initiative, which has been almost fully implemented since 2012.[6] Moreover, in adopting the two telephone indicators under the technology target, one for fixed-telephone lines (8.14) and one for mobile-cellular subscriptions (8.15), the MDGs did not foresee the global explosion in cell phone use and the declining importance of fixed-telephone lines over time. In short, the successors to the Goal 8 targets and their indicators should be periodically reviewed for continuing relevance and interest.

Fourth, the efforts to attain the MDGs should not be confused with the broader and long-standing international commitment to foster the development—or, more precisely, the sustainable development—of the developing countries. Goal 8 embodied a mixture of policy targets that were relevant to development per se, but would not directly advance any of the individual goals. For example, the case can be made that extending duty-free and quota-free (DFQF) access to developed-country markets of the exports of the least developed countries (LDCs) would better enable LDCs to mobilize tax resources for promoting domestic health and education, and would raise the income of the workers and farmers in the exporting industries. But an additional policy commitment is required to apply the additional public resources to health and education spending, and it may well be that the producers benefiting from additional exports are not among the poor or hungry of the country's population. The DFQF policy is nevertheless well worth implementing, but as a support for development in general. It is too many steps removed from actions for attaining the MDGs to count as a means of implementation of any specific MDG or of the MDGs as a whole. Indeed, in the Monterrey Consensus on Financing for Development the international community has adopted a comprehensive set of domestic and international

---

6 Since the end of 2012, only 4 of the 39 eligible countries had not reached the completion point and one has remained between decision point and completion point (see the debt sustainability chapter below for additional Heavily Indebted Poor Countries (HIPC) Initiative details).

policies for boosting development of the developing countries.[7] The follow-up to Monterrey needs to be nurtured as an essential development-promoting complement to MDG-related actions.

The Monterrey process

An intergovernmental, inter-institutional and multi-stakeholder process called "financing for development" (FfD) began at the United Nations in 1997. The focus of FfD was not the MDGs, which were only adopted late in the FfD process; the focus was development itself. It was assumed that developing countries who realized their development aspirations would most likely also attain the MDGs, or have had the capacity to do so, as well as implement a broader national economic, social and environmental agenda.

After five years of FfD discussions, the international community adopted the Monterrey Consensus on Financing for Development in 2002. The Consensus did not attempt to fit its policy commitments into the emerging international practice of stating policy commitments as goals—goals that comprised targets with fixed dates for achievement and indicators to measure the rate of implementation. The Consensus contained some quantitative commitments, which could be considered similar to targets (such as the agreed need for a "substantial increase" in ODA); there were also promises to seek consensus in various other negotiating forums (as in increasing the voice and participation of developing countries in decision-making in the Bretton Woods institutions). Most importantly, Governments understood that they were making political commitments in Monterrey, and, indeed, follow-up action to implement a number of the promised actions soon followed. Those negotiations did not always end in agreement and the pace of action and enthusiasm eroded as time passed, but a number of the promises were realized.[8]

The FfD discussions were unique in that they succeeded in bringing together a broad array of stakeholders. Governments, international financial and trade organizations, finance, trade and foreign ministries, civil society organizations and participants from the private financial sector collaboratively developed the Monterrey Consensus, which Governments then adopted under United Nations auspices. The Consensus embodied a comprehensive development cooperation strategy that included policy actions to be taken by developing and developed countries at the national level, as well as in collaboration with the international organizations through which they participated in a wide range of policy areas—from domestic to globally systemic economic governance; from trade to international investment; from more stable international financial flows to resolution of sovereign debt difficulties; from more effective domestic tax and expenditure policy in developing countries to strengthened international cooperation on tax matters; from adopting policies in traditional areas of development cooperation, as on increasing the volume and effectiveness of ODA, to agreeing to investigate

---

7   See Report of the International Conference on Financing for Development, Monterrey, Mexico, 18–22 March 2002 (A/CONF.198/11), chap. 1, resolution 1, annex.
8   See Barry Herman, "The politics of inclusion in the Monterrey process," UN/DESA Working Paper No. 23 (ST/ESA/2006/DWP/23), April 2006, New York: Department of Economic and Social Affairs of the United Nations Secretariat.

new policy possibilities, whether in the form of innovative sources of financing for development or devising a new sovereign debt workout mechanism.

By focusing on *development*, which implicitly entails economically, socially and environmentally sustainable development, the Monterrey Consensus addressed the full scope of domestic and international policies needed for development. It embodied sincere pledges to work collectively on a range of issues, but it was also pragmatic, not promising outcomes beyond what Governments were willing to work on. It was seen, in effect, as a stocktaking step in a continuing broad process of global collaboration that belonged jointly to the United Nations, the International Monetary Fund, the World Bank and the World Trade Organization, as well as to other specialized institutions and organizations of the global development community.

Towards a post-2015 global partnership for development

Efforts to achieve the MDGs will continue unabated until their target year of 2015. Meanwhile, the United Nations has committed to developing a set of sustainable development goals (SDGs) to inspire and guide international development efforts after 2015. As recommended at the United Nations Conference on Sustainable Development (Rio+20), an Open Working Group of the General Assembly has been working to develop proposals for a set of SDGs to succeed the MDGs (General Assembly decision 67/555). At the time of writing the present report, the Open Working Group was completing its proposal.[9]

A parallel intergovernmental discussion is also taking place at the United Nations, which addresses the financing of sustainable development as a whole. These discussions are taking place in the Intergovernmental Committee of Experts on Sustainable Development Financing, which the General Assembly created in June 2013 (General Assembly decision 67/559). Like the Open Working Group, this Committee had also been proposed at Rio+20—in this case, to prepare a report "proposing options on an effective sustainable development financing strategy" (General Assembly resolution 66/288, annex, para. 255),[10] which is due at the same time as the report of the Open Working Group, in September 2014. At that time, Member States will engage in an intergovernmental process to elaborate a post-2015 development agenda with SDGs at its core. The agenda is expected to be adopted at a United Nations summit meeting of Heads of State and Government in September 2015 (General Assembly resolution 68/6).

The General Assembly has also decided to hold a third International Conference on Financing for Development in Addis Ababa, Ethiopia, in July 2015 (General Assembly resolution 68/204). This conference is expected to forge consensus on a renewed global partnership for development, underpinned by a holistic and comprehensive financing framework for the mobilization of resources from a variety of sources and the effective use of financing required for the achievement of

---

9   Readers may follow the work of the Open Working Group on its website, available from http://sustainabledevelopment.un.org/owg.html.

10   Although this Committee meets behind closed doors, information about its activities is reported on its website, available from http://sustainabledevelopment.un.org/index.php?menu=1558.

sustainable development. The report of the Expert Committee will thus provide opportune input into the FfD conference. The outcome of the conference will, in turn, constitute an important contribution to and support the implementation of the post-2015 development agenda. The meeting will also be especially germane as the major stakeholders include the relevant multilateral institutions and the representatives of finance, trade and foreign ministries of Governments, as well as civil society and financial industry specialists. The FfD conference aims to bring together official decision makers to deliberate and decide upon specific policy initiatives that they would then be expected to undertake, as they did when they initiated the process in Monterrey, Mexico, in 2002.

There is a final point to make as Governments and international institutions begin to prepare for these major undertakings. The outcomes of the conferences and meetings will be negotiated documents that will not embody the mutual legal obligations of treaties, but rather the moral obligations of United Nations resolutions. Hence, a participatory evaluation and review framework to measure progress in the post-2015 development agenda and to track actions of all stakeholders will be critical. The 2014 meeting of the High-level Political Forum on Sustainable Development will discuss how best to conduct regular reviews on the follow-up and implementation of commitments and objectives of the post-2015 development agenda. However, further work is also needed to find ways to enhance local, national, regional and global accountability. The transition to a universal development agenda also requires a move towards a more integrated mode of policymaking and implementation.

The Secretary-General has called for renewing the global partnership for development as part of the post-2015 development agenda. Thus, an overarching political commitment to global development is required to forge such a renewed partnership. Clearly, the development community is intently focused on elaborating and preparing for the post-2015 development agenda. However, the political will and momentum to deliver on development cooperation commitments continues to lag, based on trends reported in the present series of reports. As 2015 draws closer, it is imperative that global leaders step forward to rally the public and the development community to join together and take the essential collective actions on the long-accepted need to eradicate global poverty, raise global living standards and sustain the global environment. The global partnership for development needs and deserves strong political revitalization.

Official development assistance

Positive developments in 2013 have helped to alleviate concerns about recent reductions in official development assistance (ODA). The highest volume ever recorded, $135 billion,[1] was reached in 2013. Much of this recovery was due to a 7 per cent increase in multilateral aid and a 25 per cent increase in aid for humanitarian emergencies. Despite an increase of aid to least developed countries (LDCs), preliminary data show an important decrease in bilateral aid to sub-Saharan Africa. In addition, indicators to monitor development cooperation effectiveness have not shown significant improvement overall. Moreover, forward spending plans of major donors do not indicate a significant growth in ODA flows. Thus, developments in the past year only partly ease the challenges facing the global partnership for development.

Update of commitments

At the special event on the Millennium Development Goals (MDGs), organized by the President of the United Nations General Assembly on 25 September 2013, Member States called for the urgent implementation of all commitments under the global partnership for development so that all gaps identified by the MDG Gap Task Force may be overcome. Specifically, United Nations Member States emphasized the need to accelerate progress towards reaching the target of disbursing the equivalent of 0.7 per cent of donor gross national income (GNI) to developing countries as ODA by 2015, and specifically 0.15 to 0.20 per cent for LDCs (General Assembly resolution 68/6).

Donors are urged to implement commitments

At the Group of Eight Summit, held in Lough Erne, Northern Ireland, in June 2013, member countries reaffirmed their commitment to sustainable global food and nutrition security. In doing so, they noted that they had now met their financial pledges made at L'Aquila in 2009 and committed to completing disbursements. They also reaffirmed their commitment to the New Alliance for Food Security and Nutrition; and to the Comprehensive Africa Agriculture Development Programme (CAADP) as the guiding framework for agricultural transformation in Africa, and recognized the New Alliance as a means to increase private sector investment in support of CAADP Country Investment Plans.[2]

In December 2013, a global coalition of developed and developing countries pledged a record $52 billion in financing over the next three years to the World Bank's International Development Association, the fund for the world's poorest countries. The coalition agreed that one focus must be to help stabilize the situation

---

1 All monetary amounts are expressed in United States dollars, except where otherwise indicated.
2 Group of Eight Leaders' Communiqué, Lough Erne, Northern Ireland, June 2013. Available from https://www.gov.uk/government/uploads/system/uploads/attachment_data/file/207771/Lough_Erne_2013_G8_Leaders_Communique.pdf.

in fragile and conflict-affected countries. This replenishment will concentrate on private sector mobilization and investments in climate change and gender equality.[3]

Two important initiatives to
strengthen development
cooperation were met
in 2014

Two multi-stakeholder efforts aimed at strengthening the effectiveness of development cooperation also had important meetings in 2014. First, the High-level Meeting of the Global Partnership for Effective Development Cooperation (GPEDC) was held in Mexico City in April 2014. This meeting brought together development leaders from over 150 countries, 70 international organizations, numerous civil society organizations, philanthropic foundations, local governments, the private sector and parliamentarians to review global progress in making development cooperation more effective and to agree on actions that will further boost development impact. The meeting's communiqué, Building Towards an Inclusive Post-2015 Development Agenda, recognizes the need to muster further political will to sustain progress and action for shared development beyond 2015, and to strengthen the focus on tangible, country-level results and opportunities for all.[4] The high-level meeting identified ways to further advance development cooperation in new areas of work, including mobilizing domestic resources and engaging the private sector as a key partner in development, while emphasizing the relevance of knowledge sharing, South-South and triangular cooperation, as well as the important role of middle-income countries in global development efforts. The participants also took stock of progress and challenges in implementing principles for effective development cooperation agreed in 2011 at the Fourth High-level Forum on Aid Effectiveness in Busan, Republic of Korea, as measured against a set of 10 global indicators. Stakeholders of the GPEDC agreed to work in synergy and cooperation with the United Nations Development Cooperation Forum (DCF) and others.

The DCF will have met in New York in July 2014, under the auspices of the Economic and Social Council, after this report has been published. It will bring together the full range of development cooperation actors, including high-level representatives of developed and developing countries, international organizations, civil society, philanthropic foundations, the private sector and other development leaders. The July meeting marks the culmination of a two-year preparatory process of a series of country-led, multi-stakeholder, high-level symposiums and dialogues. Participants will provide critical input into the post-2015 preparatory process on the future of development cooperation and address the essential role that ODA could play in the post-2015 financing mix. The Forum is expected to generate policy recommendations on how development cooperation will have to change to support implementation of a post-2015 development agenda, and what a renewed global partnership for development could look like and how it should work in practice. It will also continue to build synergistic relationships with the GPEDC.[5] The Forum will call for a robust global monitoring and accountability framework for development cooperation commitments so as to engage all actors on a level playing field.

---

3 See "World Bank's fight against extreme poverty gets record support", press release, 17 December 2013, available from http://www.worldbank.org/en/news/press-release/2013/12/17/world-bank-fight-extreme-poverty-record-support.

4 Mexico High-level Meeting Communiqué, 16 April 2014, available from http://effectivecooperation.org/wordpress/wp-content/uploads/2014/05/FinalConsensusMexicoHLMCommunique.pdf.

5 See information sheet on the 2014 Development Cooperation Forum, available from http://www.un.org/en/ecosoc/newfunct/pdf13/2014_dcf_one-pager.pdf.

This will be done through existing global, regional, national and local accountability mechanisms that build on findings of the third global accountability survey and other initiatives of the DCF. The Forum's conclusions will provide an input into the work of the Open Working Group on Sustainable Development Goals and the third International Conference on Financing for Development, to be held in 2015.

ODA delivery and prospects

After two consecutive years of falling volumes, net official development aid rose 6.1 per cent in 2013 in real terms to reach the highest level ever recorded, despite the continuing pressure on budgets in some member countries of the Organization for Economic Cooperation and Development (OECD) since the global economic crisis. Total net ODA flows from the member countries of the OECD Development Assistance Committee (DAC) amounted to $134.8 billion in 2013 in current dollars, up from $126.9 billion in 2012 (figure 1).

Record ODA levels were reached…

Figure 1
Main components of ODA of DAC members, 2000–2013 *(billions of 2012 dollars)*

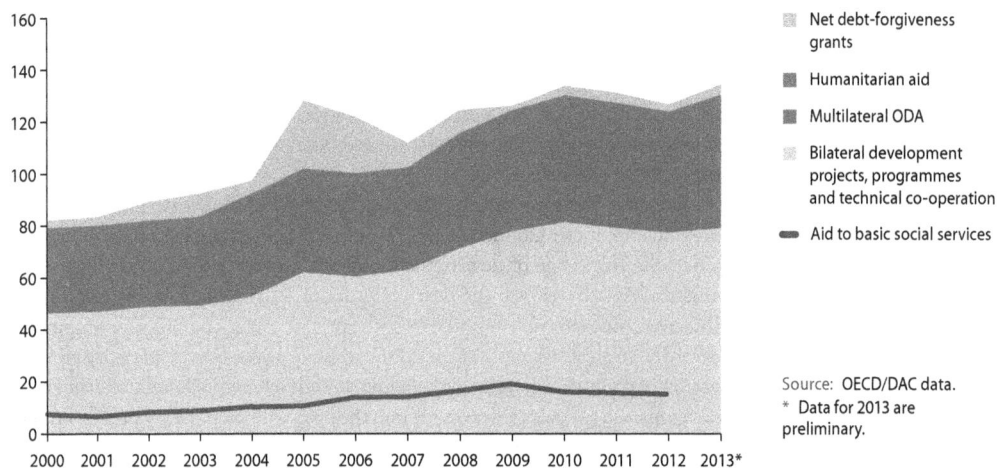

Net debt-forgiveness grants

Humanitarian aid

Multilateral ODA

Bilateral development projects, programmes and technical co-operation

Aid to basic social services

Source: OECD/DAC data.
* Data for 2013 are preliminary.

Preliminary estimates show that much of the 2013 increase in volume came from ODA contributions to multilateral institutions—which increased from $38 billion the previous year to approximately $41 billion in constant prices and exchange rates—and humanitarian aid, which increased from about $8 billion to $11 billion. Net aid for core bilateral projects and programmes, which represents about 60 per cent of the total, rose from $77 billion to $79 billion in real terms. Debt-relief grants increased from $3 billion to $4 billion.

In contrast to the previous year, when most donor countries decreased their development aid flows, net ODA rose in 17 out of the 28 DAC countries,[6] with

---

6 The Czech Republic, Iceland, Poland, Slovakia and Slovenia became Organization for Economic Cooperation and Development/Development Assistance Committee (OECD/DAC) members in 2013. Aid flows from these countries are included in this analysis.

the largest increases in volume recorded in Iceland, Italy, Japan, Norway and the United Kingdom of Great Britain and Northern Ireland. The United Kingdom had explicitly expressed its intention to increase aid to 0.7 per cent of GNI, and met the target for the first time in 2013. The largest donors in order of volume were the United States of America, the United Kingdom, Germany, Japan and France. The United States remained the largest donor by volume with net ODA flows of $31.5 billion, an increase of 1.3 per cent in real terms from 2012, mostly due to humanitarian aid and support for fighting HIV/AIDS. Denmark, Luxembourg, Norway, Sweden and the United Kingdom met the United Nations target to disburse the equivalent of 0.7 per cent of their GNI in aid (figure 2). For the first time since 1974, aid from the Netherlands fell below the United Nations target. Aid fell in the remaining 11 DAC countries, with the biggest decreases (as a percentage of the donor's GNI) in Canada, France and Portugal.

Figure 2
ODA of DAC members, 2000, 2012 and 2013 (*percentage of GNI*)

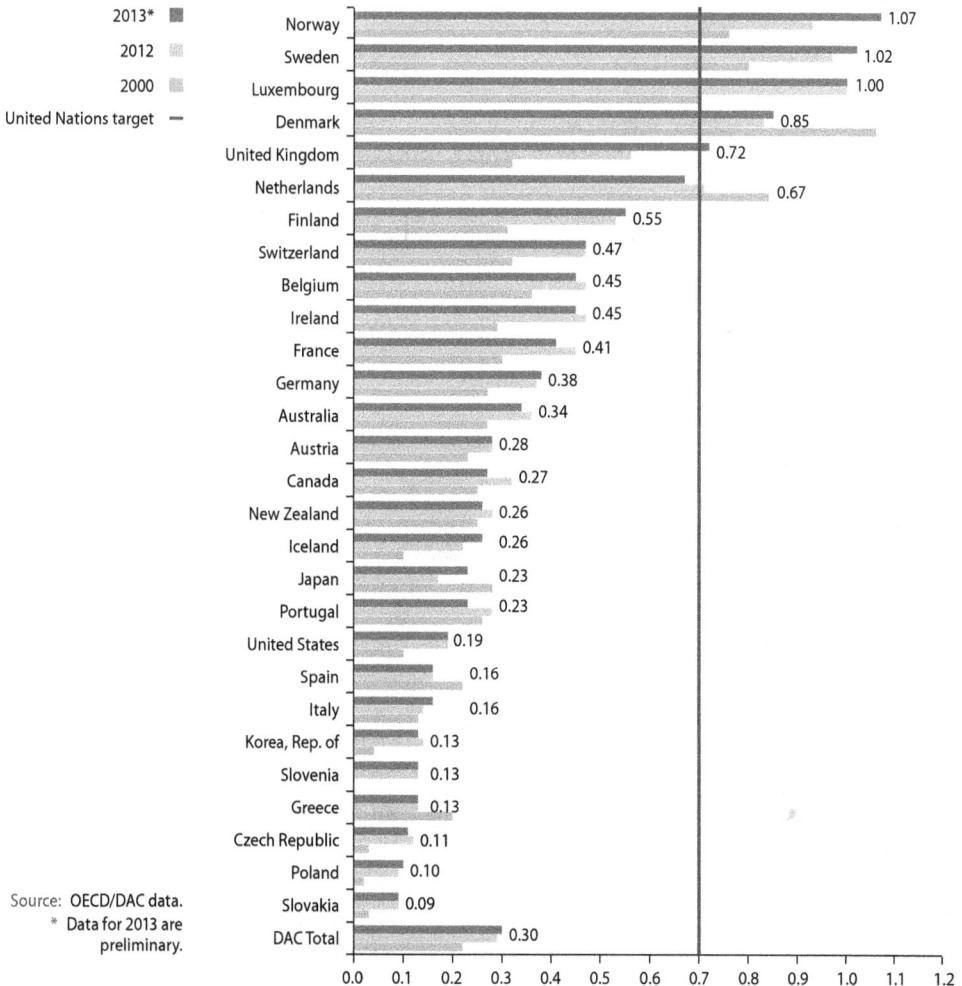

Legend:
2013* ■
2012
2000
United Nations target —

Country	Value
Norway	1.07
Sweden	1.02
Luxembourg	1.00
Denmark	0.85
United Kingdom	0.72
Netherlands	0.67
Finland	0.55
Switzerland	0.47
Belgium	0.45
Ireland	0.45
France	0.41
Germany	0.38
Australia	0.34
Austria	0.28
Canada	0.27
New Zealand	0.26
Iceland	0.26
Japan	0.23
Portugal	0.23
United States	0.19
Spain	0.16
Italy	0.16
Korea, Rep. of	0.13
Slovenia	0.13
Greece	0.13
Czech Republic	0.11
Poland	0.10
Slovakia	0.09
DAC Total	0.30

Source: OECD/DAC data.
* Data for 2013 are preliminary.

0.0 0.1 0.2 0.3 0.4 0.5 0.6 0.7 0.8 0.9 1.0 1.1 1.2

The overall increase in ODA has meant a narrowing of the gap between the United Nations target of disbursing 0.7 per cent of donor GNI and the actual flows. In 2013, the combined DAC donors' ODA was equivalent to 0.30 per cent of their combined GNI, leaving a delivery gap of 0.40 per cent of GNI, marginally less than the 0.41 per cent of 2012 (table 1). In order to reach the United Nations target that would now amount to $315 billion (in 2012 dollars), DAC donors would need to increase their annual disbursements by $180 billion.

...and the gap to reach the United Nations target narrowed...

Table 1
Delivery gaps in aid commitments by DAC donors, 2012 and 2013

		Percentage of GNI	Billions of current dollars
Total ODA	United Nations target	0.7	314.6
	Delivery in 2013	0.3	134.8
	Gap in 2013	0.4	179.8
ODA to LDCs	United Nations target	0.15–0.20	67.6–90.1
	Delivery in 2012	0.09	40.5
	Gap in 2012	0.06–0.11	27.0–49.5

Source: UN/DESA, based on OECD/DAC data.

Although aid flows are not easy to predict, especially in times of weak economic situations, some indication can be extracted from an annual survey of donor spending plans by the OECD/DAC on country programmable aid (CPA), which is the portion of aid that donors programme for individual countries. It attempts to capture the volume of flows actually received by developing countries from both bilateral and multilateral donors.[7] The 2014 DAC Survey on Donors' Forward Spending Plans projects that CPA will increase 2.4 per cent in real terms in 2014, owing to continued increases by a few DAC donors and multilateral agencies, but is expected to remain roughly unchanged beyond 2014. In 2013, global CPA levels grew 10.2 per cent in real terms, rising more quickly than the overall trend.[8]

...but aid is expected to remain unchanged

Allocation by region and country group[9]

Preliminary estimates show that bilateral aid to sub-Saharan Africa was $26.2 billion in 2013, a decrease of 4.0 per cent in real terms from 2012. Much of this decrease was due to lower levels of debt relief, which had been relatively high in 2012 due to assistance to Côte d'Ivoire. Bilateral aid to the African continent as a whole fell by 5.6 per cent, to $28.9 billion.

Aid to Africa fell...

---

7 Country programmable aid (CPA) excludes items of official development assistance (ODA) that are not being transferred, such as debt relief and in-donor costs (including administrative costs, student costs, refugee costs and development-awareness spending). However, CPA does not provide a fully accurate picture of the receipts either, as it excludes some types of aid that actually involve a resource transfer, such as humanitarian aid, aid through local governments and food aid.

8 Organization for Economic Cooperation and Development, "Outlook on aid: survey on donors' forward spending plans 2014–2017," forthcoming.

9 Although some preliminary data disaggregated into regions and country groups are available for 2013, more detailed information is available only for 2012. Thus, most of the analysis in this section refers to 2012.

...but increased to LDCs

However, net bilateral ODA to LDCs rose 12.3 per cent in real terms to about $30 billion, mostly owing to the exceptional debt relief extended to Myanmar in 2013, according to estimates. The increased bilateral flows in 2013 partly reflect the fact that aid to LDCs from DAC donors had dropped in 2012. It declined 7.6 per cent in real terms from $43.9 billion in 2011 to $40.5 billion in 2012 (in 2012 dollars).[10] This fall had been particularly worrisome as it was much larger than the one to developing countries as a whole.

Some LDCs depend heavily on ODA as their primary source of external and public financing. ODA still represents over 70 per cent of total external financing in LDCs. In addition, their capacity to attract other forms of external financing remains limited, with access to foreign direct investment and other external financing being modest and usually more volatile.[11] The median of the ratio of ODA to government revenues, although decreasing, still stood at about 60 per cent for LDCs as a whole.[12] The LDCs also display the highest incidence of extreme poverty among all groups of countries, with about half of their population living on less than $1.25 day.[13]

Previous progress made towards the United Nations target of ODA to LDCs suffered a reversal in 2012, the latest year for which disaggregated data is available. As a share of DAC GNI, aid to LDCs almost doubled from 0.06 per cent in 2000 to 0.11 per cent in 2010, but dropped to 0.09 per cent in 2012. The gap between DAC donors' ODA flows to LDCs and the lower bound United Nations target of 0.15 per cent has thus widened to 0.06 per cent of donor GNI (table 1). This puts the shortfall in LDC aid in 2012 at $27 billion (in 2012 dollars). Only 8 of the 28 DAC donors (Denmark, Finland, Ireland, Luxembourg, the Netherlands, Norway, Sweden and the United Kingdom) met or exceeded the lower bound United Nations target of 0.15 per cent of GNI to LDCs (figure 3). Nineteen DAC members reduced their contributions to LDCs in 2012 as a percentage of their GNI, compared to 21 members in 2011. Belgium, which had surpassed the target's upper bound for three consecutive years since 2009, reduced its ODA to LDCs by 0.06 percentage points, from 0.20 to 0.14 per cent of its GNI in 2012. Similarly, Portugal reduced its flows to LDCs from 0.15 in 2011 to 0.09 per cent of its GNI in 2012. Sweden also reduced aid to LDCs by 0.07 percentage points, but its overall contribution of 0.29 per cent remained far above the upper bound of the United Nations target, which is set at 0.20 per cent.

---

10 Total ODA to least developed countries (LDCs) includes an imputation of the share of donor multilateral contributions that are devoted to LDCs.
11 Organization for Economic Cooperation and Development, "The where of development finance: towards better targeting of concessional finance," DCD/DAC(2013)29, Paris, 2013.
12 Department of Economic and Social Affairs of the United Nations Secretariat (UN/DESA) estimates based on 2011 data from the World Bank's World Development Indicators.
13 United Nations, "State of the least developed countries 2013: follow up of the implementation of the Istanbul Programme of Action for the least developed countries", New York: United Nations Office of the High Representative for the Least Developed Countries, Landlocked Developing Countries and Small Island Developing States, 2013.

Figure 3
ODA of DAC donors provided to least developed countries, 2000, 2011 and 2012
(*percentage of GNI*)

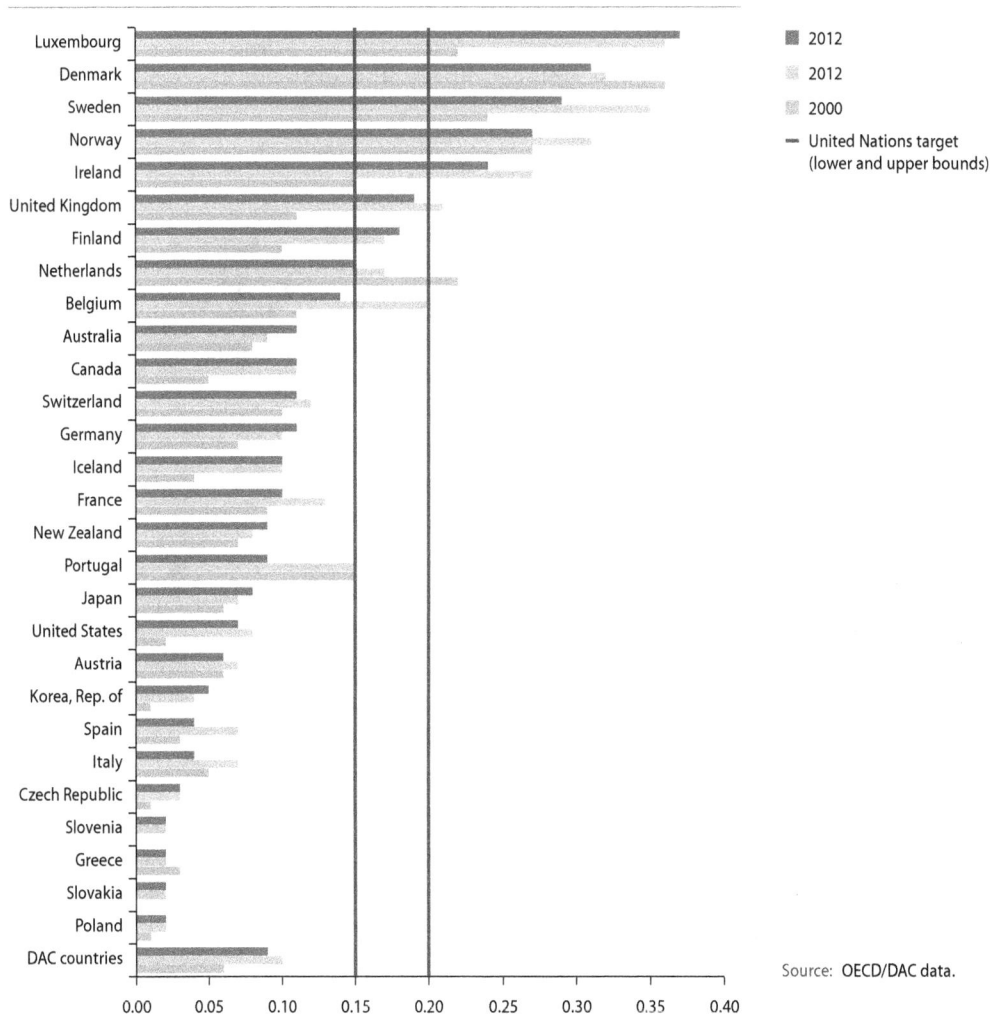

Landlocked developing countries (LLDCs) and small island developing States (SIDS) are considered international priorities for assistance because of their geographical situations. However, aid flows to LLDCs have stagnated between $26 billion and $27 billion from 2010 to 2012 (in 2012 dollars) (figure 4). Aid to SIDS continued to fall for a second consecutive year in 2012, from $5.1 billion in 2011 to $4.7 billion in 2012. This represented 3.3 per cent of the GNI of the SIDS, a decrease of more than half a percentage point. The Third International Conference on Small Island Developing States, to be held from 1 to 4 September 2014 in Apia, Samoa, and the Second United Nations Conference on Landlocked Developing Countries, to be held in Vienna from 3 to 5 November 2014, should address the gaps in official support for these groups of countries that remain a special cause for concern in view of their unique and particular vulnerabilities.

Figure 4
Total ODA received by priority groups of countries, 2000–2012 (*billions of 2012 dollars*)

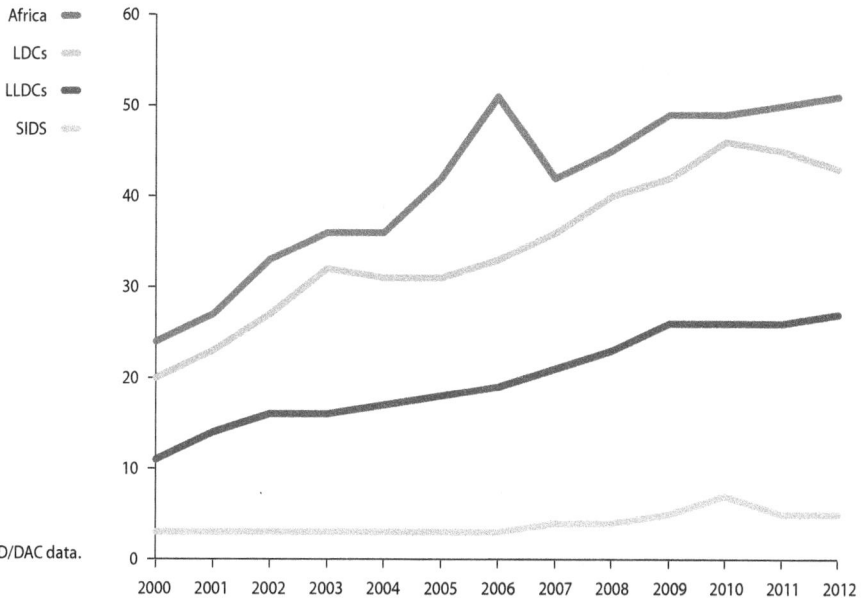

Africa
LDCs
LLDCs
SIDS

Source: OECD/DAC data.

The 2014 DAC Survey on Donors' Forward Spending Plans suggests a continuation of the worrying trend of declines in CPA to LDCs and other low-income countries (LICs), in particular those in Africa. CPA to LDCs and LICs is set to decrease by 5 per cent, reflecting reduced access to grant resources on which these countries highly depend. Some Asian countries may see increases, however, such that overall allocations to Asia are expected to equal those to Africa by 2017.

Allocation of aid continues to be skewed...

Aid continues to be heavily concentrated in a small number of countries. The top 20 recipients in 2012 (out of 158 countries and territories) accounted for 53 per cent of total ODA (table 2). Despite an overall decrease in aid flows, Afghanistan continues to be the largest recipient of aid, not only among LLDCs, but all developing countries, receiving approximately $6.8 billion in 2012. Otherwise, the country composition has changed somewhat in 2012 compared with 2011. The Democratic Republic of the Congo fell from being the second highest aid recipient in 2011, when it received exceptional debt relief, to the fifth in 2012, after experiencing an almost 47 per cent decrease in aid.[14] Close to two thirds of the increase of ODA to the LDCs during the past 10 years has gone to only four countries: Afghanistan, Democratic Republic of the Congo, Ethiopia and Sudan.

---

14 In addition, flows to Viet Nam increased 16.5 per cent, making it the second highest aid recipient in 2012. Pakistan fell from being the fifth to the twelfth highest aid recipient, while India fell from the sixth to the sixteenth position. Bangladesh moved up from being the seventeenth to being the ninth highest aid recipient and Côte d'Ivoire also moved up, from the nineteenth to the seventh position. The Democratic Republic of the Congo, Haiti, Iraq and South Africa fell out of the top twenty in 2012, while South Sudan, Egypt and the Syrian Arab Republic experienced significant increases in aid flows of 46 per cent, 355 per cent and 403 per cent, respectively.

Table 2
Top aid recipients in 2012 (*millions of 2011 dollars*)

	2002 ODA receipts	2012 ODA receipts	Change from 2011 to 2012 (*percentage*)	GNI per capita in 2012
Afghanistan	2032	6777	-2	680
Viet Nam	2026	4191	17	1550
Ethiopia	2063	3311	-7	380
Turkey	423	3237	2	10830
Democratic Republic of the Congo	1865	2950	-47	230
United Republic of Tanzania	2069	2881	18	570
Côte d'Ivoire	1800	2762	92	1220
Kenya	590	2698	9	860
Bangladesh	1428	2191	47	840
Mozambique	3669	2147	3	510
West Bank and Gaza	1562	2059	-16	..
Pakistan	3183	2042	-42	1260
Nigeria	443	1938	10	1440
Egypt	1830	1884	355	2980
Ghana	1059	1849	2	1550
India	2613	1691	-48	1550
Syrian Arab Republic	101	1685	403	..
Uganda	1135	1684	7	480
South Sudan	0	1583	46	790
Morocco	600	1557	7	2960
Top 10 total	17965	33145	..	..
Share in total ODA (percentage)	24	34	..	..
Top 20 total	30491	51116	..	..
Share in total ODA (percentage)	41	53	..	..

Source: UN/DESA, based on OECD/DAC and World Bank data.

Although the norms and priorities contained in international agreements should help guide the allocations, aid is not necessarily allocated according to the needs or absorptive capacity of the recipient country. Bilateral aid agencies sometimes base their decisions on non-developmental concerns, which are influenced by specific contexts and historical relationships. A DAC survey has identified the following seven countries as still underaided or "aid orphans" in 2012, according to needs- and performance-based criteria:[15] Guinea, Madagascar, Nepal, Gambia, Togo, Niger and Sierra Leone. Guinea, Madagascar and Nepal were identified as aid orphans during the entire survey period from 2006 and 2012; the Gambia and Togo for 6 years; the Niger for 5 of these years; and Sierra Leone for the last two years. Bangladesh, which was a top aid recipient in 2012, was identified as an aid orphan between 2009 and 2011.

...and many countries remain underaided

---

15 Organization for Economic Cooperation and Development, "OECD-DAC development brief: where do we stand on the aid orphans?", Paris, 2014.

Aid modalities

To qualify as ODA, a financial transfer or technical assistance programme must not only promote the economic development and welfare of developing countries, but must also be either a grant or a loan, conveying a "grant element" of at least 25 per cent.[16] The latest data from the OECD shows that the average share of grants in total ODA during the period 2011–2012 was 85.4 per cent, only slightly lower than in 2010–2011.[17] The countries that had a below-average share were France, Germany, Japan, Portugal and the Republic of Korea. The average share of grants in bilateral ODA was 79.9 per cent.

Another characteristic of ODA is that in some instances, recipient Governments are free to select the aid programmes of any implementing organizations they wish; in others, they must employ entities tied to the donor Government. Progress towards untying aid varies considerably among donor countries. A number of donors have gradually untied their aid over the past decade, while others, such as Austria, Germany and Greece, reversed earlier progress. In 2012, only Australia, Iceland, Ireland, Norway and the United Kingdom had untied 100 per cent of their aid (figure 5). In Greece, the share of untied aid stood at 6.4 per cent in 2012, a significant decrease from 93.2 per cent in 2011. All DAC donors with the exception of Austria, the Czech Republic, Greece, the Republic of Korea and Portugal have untied more than half of their aid.

More aid was untied   There has been some progress in fulfilling the 2001 DAC recommendation to untie ODA to the LDCs to the greatest extent possible. In 2012, 83 per cent of DAC bilateral aid to the LDCs was untied, excluding administrative costs, a 2 percentage-point improvement since 2011 (figure 6).

Acknowledging the changes in the new global development landscape and the need to modernize its statistical system to better reflect these changes, the DAC decided to take the following steps at its high-level meeting on 4 and 5 December 2012: elaborate a proposal for a new headline measure of total official support for development (TOSD) to complement ODA, and support the post-2015 sustainable development agenda; explore ways of capturing the full extent of official donor effort and also provide a more comprehensive picture of external development finance from the recipients' perspective; and, in view of the above, put forward proposals to modernize the ODA concept.[18]

To address concerns resulting from divergences in DAC members' practices with respect to assessing the concessionality of loans, the DAC also agreed to establish a clear, quantitative definition of "concessional in character" for ODA loans by 2015. The current quantitative test of having a 25 per cent grant element, using a 10 per cent discount rate for scoring a loan as ODA, has allowed some DAC donors to extend loans at little or no direct budgetary cost, given the pre-

---

16 In fact, the grant element of ODA to LDCs was 99.3 per cent (2011–2012 average), while that of total ODA was 95.2 per cent, reflecting that most ODA is in the form of grants; the grant element of ODA loans ranged from 46.0 to 90.3 per cent; see also, Organization for Economic Cooperation and Development, "Statistics on resource flows to developing countries," table 20, available from http://www.oecd.org/dac/stats/statisticsonresourceflowstodevelopingcountries.htm.

17 Ibid.

18 See the DAC high-level meeting communiqué, available from http://www.oecd.org/dac/externalfinancingfordevelopment/documentupload/HLM%20Communique%202012%20final%20ENGLISH.pdf.

vailing financial market conditions. This casts doubt on the ODA measurement as a reliable indicator of donor effort. The DAC is currently investigating several options for resolving this issue.

Figure 5
Share of untied bilateral ODA of DAC members, 2011 and 2012 (*percentage*)

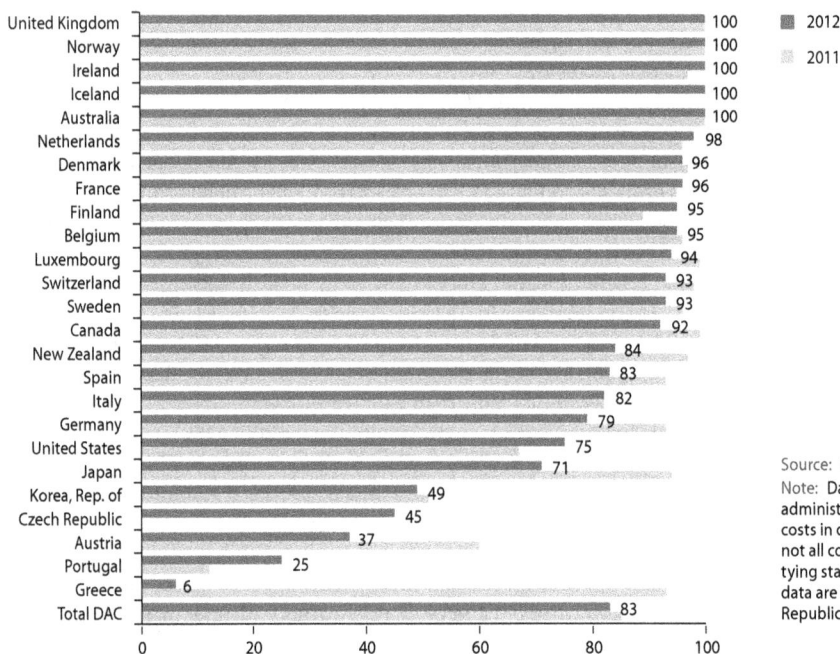

Source: OECD/DAC data.
Note: Data exclude administrative and refugee costs in donor countries, as not all countries reported the tying status of this item; no data are available for the Czech Republic and Iceland in 2011.

Figure 6
Share of untied bilateral ODA of DAC members to LDCs, 2012 (*percentage*)

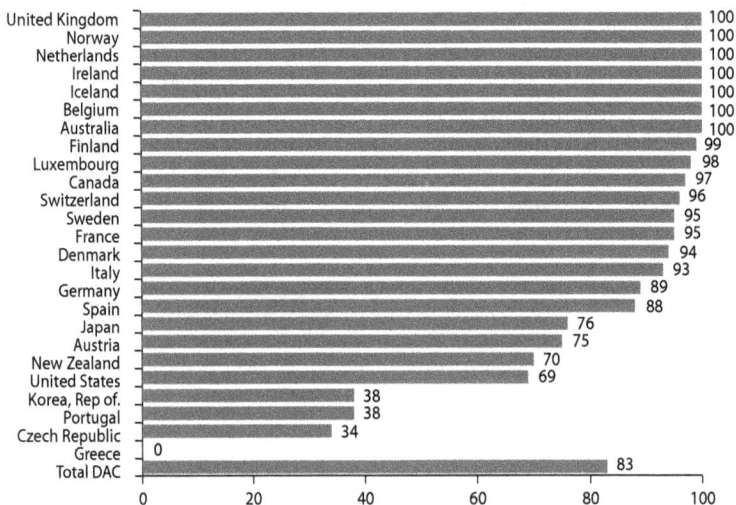

Source: OECD/DAC data.
Note: Data exclude administrative costs, to follow the DAC recommendation on untying ODA to the LDCs.

Other sources of concessional development finance

Financing from non-DAC
donors and the private
sector continues to be
important

In addition to ODA from DAC donor Governments, an increasing number of other official sources are providing concessional development financing. However, this assistance may be provided on different terms and conditions than ODA. Several of the providing countries report to the OECD,[19] which then compiles the data on these flows according to DAC specifications. The monitored flows amounted to $6.5 billion in 2012, which represented a fall of 27 per cent from a high of $8.9 billion in 2011 (figure 7). Turkey has gradually increased its development flows to $2.5 billion to become the largest donor among the reporting non-DAC countries, surpassing Saudi Arabia, whose flows shrank to one fourth of their level in 2011, falling from $5.5 billion to $1.3 billion in 2012 (directed almost exclusively to Arab countries). Most of the increase in Turkish aid has been in the form of assistance given to Syrian refugees in Turkey and support to North African countries following events surrounding the Arab Spring.[20]

In addition, estimates have been made of gross concessional flows from other key partners.[21] OECD estimates that China, India and South Africa disbursed about $2.6 billion, $605 million and $152 million, respectively, in bilateral funds in 2012.[22] The estimates also show that Brazil disbursed about $500 million in total "ODA-like" flows (as determined by the OECD) in 2010.

Private organizations also provide concessional financing. In 2012, total net private grants from non-governmental organizations and other private voluntary agencies amounted to $29.8 billion, down from $32 billion in 2011.[23] However, it must be noted that the purpose of these grants and their relationship to development vary greatly. One of the most prominent sources of development financing among the private organizations is the Bill and Melinda Gates Foundation, which reports disbursements of about $2.7 billion in 2011 for development, 34 per cent more than in 2010. About two thirds of these flows were directed to Africa. Two thirds of this amount was extended in grants for health purposes, including reproductive health.[24]

In addition, as mentioned above, the DAC is preparing a more comprehensive measure of the development cooperation efforts of its members—the aforementioned TOSD—to complement the ODA measure. It is intended to

---

19 For a list of non-DAC donors that report to the Organization for Economic Cooperation and Development (OECD), see http://www.oecd.org/dac/stats/non-dac-reporting.htm.

20 Organization for Economic Cooperation and Development, *Development Cooperation Report 2013: Ending Poverty*, Paris, 2013.

21 While it was agreed at the 2011 High-level Forum on Aid Effectiveness in Busan that the "nature, modalities and responsibilities that apply to South-South cooperation differ from those that apply to North-South cooperation" (Busan Partnership for Effective Development Cooperation, para. 2), international statistical methodologies for tracking South-South cooperation have thus far not been developed. Data in this paragraph pertain to DAC methodologies.

22 Organization for Economic Cooperation and Development, "Statistics on resource flows to developing countries," table 33a, Paris, available from http://www.oecd.org/dac/stats/statisticsonresourceflowstodevelopingcountries.htm.

23 Organization for Economic Cooperation and Development, "OECD statistics", available from http://stats.oecd.org/.

24 Organization for Economic Cooperation and Development, *Development Cooperation Report 2013*, op. cit., footnote 19.

provide recognition of the full range of member Governments' and other actors' efforts to support the emerging sustainable development agenda.[25]

Figure 7
Development finance from non-DAC countries reporting to the OECD, 2000–2012
(*billions of 2011 dollars*)

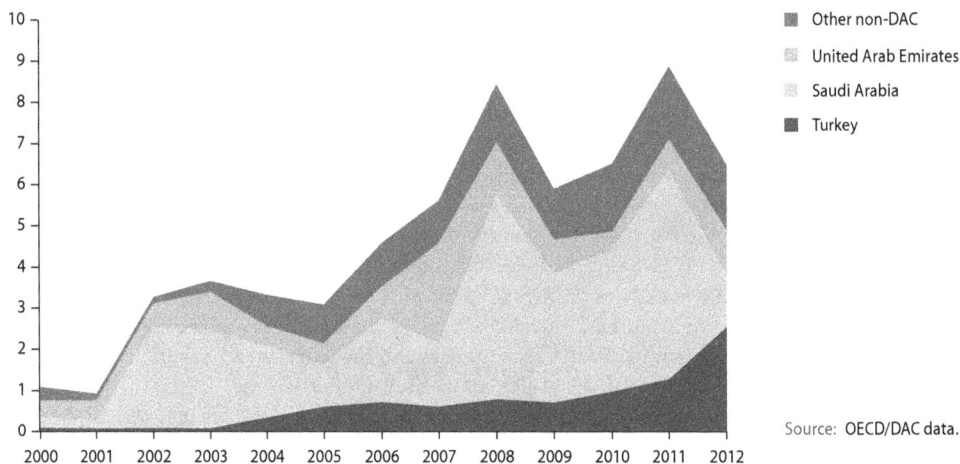

Source: OECD/DAC data.

Legend: Other non-DAC, United Arab Emirates, Saudi Arabia, Turkey

Effectiveness of development cooperation

Providers of development cooperation have long worked to improve the impact of development cooperation efforts. The DAC addressed making aid more effective as a priority in its founding document in 1961 and in periodic special efforts thereafter, including in its leadership of the Paris and Accra processes over the past decade.[26] Since 2011, the GPEDC has been committed to shifting the focus from aid effectiveness only to a broader concept of effective development cooperation with more stakeholder participation, still sustained by ODA as the main source of international development assistance. GPEDC also aims to strengthen the long-term development impact of domestic resources and provide a forum for the convergence of the efforts of all public and private development stakeholders.[27]

Similarly, United Nations Member States decided at the 2005 World Summit to create the DCF to "promote greater coherence among the development activities of different development partners" (General Assembly resolution 60/1, para. 155). The aim of the DCF and the GPEDC is to help recipient Governments sufficiently strengthen their monitoring, reporting and decision-making systems so as to take full ownership of the development cooperation programmes. In that situ-

A broader concept of development cooperation is being sought

---

25 Organization for Economic Cooperation and Development, "Modernizing the DAC's development finance statistics," DCD/DAC(2014)9, Paris, 2014.
26 See Barry Herman, "Towards a new global partnership for development: Looking backward to look forward," background study for the Ethiopia High-level Symposium for the 2014 Development Cooperation Forum, Addis Ababa, 5–7 June 2013, available from http://www.un.org/en/ecosoc/newfunct/pdf13/dcf_ethiopia_background_study.pdf, pp. 9–12.
27 Mexico High-level Meeting Communiqué, op. cit.

ation, providers would accept the use of country results frameworks and financial management systems to guide and deliver their assistance, and recipients would record assistance programmes in national budgets that are vetted by parliaments. Providers would also fully untie their assistance and disburse funds as promised in their forward spending plans. There would be greater transparency and accountability in all phases of development cooperation, including public posting of projects and programmes using a common information standard.

Another common feature of the DCF and the GPEDC is the effort to monitor the extent to which donors and aid recipients implement the policy and operational reforms that they pledged to undertake in order to make development cooperation more effective. In this regard, the Third Global Accountability Survey on Mutual Accountability for the DCF suggests that there has been some progress in implementing mutual accountability.[28] The number of countries with national aid policies in place has increased since 2011, and more recipient countries have set targets. Yet, the overall impact of national mutual accountability was considered moderate and a number of implementation challenges remain, including the adequacy of existing mechanisms to support implementation of a universal and unified post-2015 development agenda. In addition to monitoring cooperation, a recent GPEDC report provides an important focus on better enabling civil society and the private sector to contribute to development cooperation.[29]

Policy recommendations

- As Member States are accelerating their efforts to achieve the MDGs by the target year of 2015, donor Governments must accelerate their efforts to meet past commitments and achieve the United Nations target of disbursing the equivalent of 0.7 per cent of GNI in ODA to support these efforts

- Donor Governments must further increase the share of ODA to priority groups of countries, including Africa, LLDCs and SIDS, as originally committed in MDG 8, given the greater need of these countries

- Non-DAC countries and other development actors are urged to continue to provide and scale up their development cooperation

- All development actors should report openly on their activities in order to improve coordination and take advantage of possible synergies with other sources of financing

- All development actors should take the necessary action to accelerate progress in increasing country ownership and focus on results, inclusiveness, transparency and mutual accountability

- Member States are encouraged to build on the discussions at the Fourth High-level Meeting of the Development Cooperation Forum to develop a new narrative that mobilizes international effort for a more inclusive, accountable and effective development cooperation in preparation for the launch of the new development agenda post-2015

---

28 See "Accountable and effective development cooperation in a post-2015 era", background study No. 2 for the Third Global Accountability Survey on Mutual Accountability, available from http://www.un.org/en/ecosoc/newfunct/pdf13/dcf_germany_bkgd_study_2_ma_survey.pdf.

29 See Organization for Economic Cooperation and Development and United Nations Development Programme, *Making Development Cooperation More Effective: 2014 Progress Report*, Paris: OECD, 2014.

Market access (trade)

A central concern of Millennium Development Goal (MDG) 8 is to support developing countries in attaining the goals of the Millennium Declaration through economic growth, with a focus on the growth of their exports, to be supported by an open, rule-based, predictable and non-discriminatory trading system. However, growth in the volume of developing-country exports has slowed in recent years, falling from 4.3 per cent in 2012 to 3.2 per cent in 2013; it is forecast to accelerate, but only to 4.1 per cent in 2014 and 5.1 per cent in 2015.[1] This reflects, in part, the slow and uneven growth of the global economy since recovery from the Great Recession began; and while international commodity prices had earlier reflected strong global demand, those prices fell in 2013. The growth of the dollar value of developing-country exports thus slowed dramatically in 2013, growing an estimated 2.5 per cent compared with 7.6 per cent in 2012 and over 20 per cent in each of the prior two years of recovery.[2]

While conjunctural factors largely determine developing-country earnings from trade in the short run, improving the trading prospects of developing countries over the medium term was a central purpose of the Doha Round when negotiations began at the World Trade Organization (WTO) in 2001. After a decade of inconclusive negotiations, agreement on the Bali Package in 2013 delivered a certain measure of encouragement in this regard, showing that obstacles to a multilateral trade agreement can be overcome. The task remains, however, to build on that momentum so as to fully implement the agreement and to facilitate further improvement in the policy environment for promoting developing-country trade, especially for least developed countries (LDCs).

Developments in trade policy

Multilateral policy: the Bali Package

After over a decade of blocked negotiations, a breakthrough was achieved at the ninth Ministerial Conference of the WTO, held in Bali from 3 to 7 December 2013. Before the meeting, WTO members agreed to focus on a limited agenda of policy matters on which they believed they could reach agreement—and they did. Labelled the Bali Package, the agreements covered trade facilitation, agriculture, a package of decisions related to the LDCs, and a monitoring system on special and differential treatment (SDT) provisions.

The Trade Facilitation Agreement, the first multilateral agreement concluded in the WTO since its creation in 1995, contains commitments aimed at reducing trade transaction costs, increasing transparency and better harmonizing

A breakthrough in negotiations was achieved with the Bali Package

---

1 United Nations, "World economic situation and prospects as of mid-2014" (E/2014/70).
2 *World Economic Situation and Prospects 2014* (United Nations publication, Sales No. E.14.II.C.2).

customs formalities. This could, in some cases, provide a greater incentive for increased trade that would prompt further reductions in tariffs. According to a recent study, a multilateral trade facilitation agreement could induce a reduction in business costs equivalent to up to 15 per cent of present costs and raise global exports by as much as $1 trillion[3] in the most optimistic scenario.[4] In Africa, an analysis of comprehensive trade costs reveals that disproportionately high trans-action costs may not only hamper Africa's trade with the rest of the world, but also negatively affect regional integration, particularly across regional economic communities, causing what has been termed a "proximity gap".[5]

The agreement has been strongly backed by developed countries and a number of developing countries. While developing countries recognize the benefits of the agreement in reducing trade-related costs, they have expressed concerns about the costs of implementation of trade facilitation measures and the mostly voluntary nature of commitments for technical and financial support for trade facilitation. Indeed, a unique feature of the agreement is that the implementation of commitments can be modulated across three categories, one of which requires the acquisition of implementation capacity through the pro-vision of technical and financial assistance and support for capacity-building. Since the agreement's implementation relies on this condition, its implementa-tion by capacity-constrained countries—and the ensuing benefits from resulting increased trade—will depend on the readiness of donors to make the necessary commitments, which are non-binding. Furthermore, to make the agreement bet-ter support development, additional investments in transport-corridor upgrading and economic infrastructure must be put in place in a number of countries.

Regarding the second part of the Bali Package, the Doha Declaration had provided a clear mandate "to establish a fair and market-oriented trading system ... in world agricultural markets".[6] Nonetheless, comprehensive negotiations on

Some concerns regarding agriculture held by developing countries were addressed...

---

3 All monetary amounts are expressed in United Stated dollars, except where otherwise indicated.

4 See Organization for Economic Cooperation and Development, "The WTO Trade Facilitation Agreement: potential impact on trade costs", Paris, February 2014. Another study argues that a trade facilitation agreement could increase exports of developing countries by approximately $570 billion and exports of developed countries by $475 billion (Gary Clyde Hufbauer and Jeffrey J. Schott, "Payoff from the world trade agenda 2013", Washington, D.C.: Peterson Institute for International Economics, April 2013).

5 In addition, estimates by the United Nations Economic Commission for Africa indi-cate that if the establishment of the Continental Free Trade Area is complemented by trade facilitation measures, the share of intra-African trade would more than double between 2012 and 2022, from 10.2 per cent to 21.9 per cent, with associated benefits for economic diversification. See Simon Mevel and Stephen Karingi , "Deepening regional integration in Africa: a computable general equilibrium assessment of the establishment of a continental free trade area followed by a continental customs union", paper pre-sented at the Seventh African Economic Conference, Kigali, 30 October-2 November 2012; United Nations Economic Commission for Africa, *Trade Facilitation from an African Perspective*, Addis Ababa, 2013; and Giovanni Valensisi, Robert Tama Lisinge and Stephen Karingi , "Towards an assessment of the dividends and economic benefits of successfully implementing trade facilitation measures at the level of African REC", paper presented at the Post-Bali Trade Facilitation Symposium for African LDCs, Mwanza, United Republic of Tanzania, 14–16 May 2014.

6 Doha World Trade Organization Ministerial Declaration, adopted on 14 November 2001, WT/MIN(01)/DEC/1, para. 13, available from http://www.wto.org/english/ thewto_e/minist_e/min01_e/mindecl_e.htm.

the reform of the Agreement on Agriculture stalled in December 2008. The Bali Package, however, contains decisions that address some concerns voiced by developing countries. The first of these decisions prevents members from challenging public stockholding schemes for food security purposes if certain conditions are met, and mandates negotiations to permanently settle this issue over the next four years. Another decision clarifies that General Services programmes related to land reform and rural livelihoods are not subject to subsidy-reduction commitments. The third decision clarifies procedures for the administration of tariff-rate quotas (in which a quota limits how much of a commodity may be imported at a reduced tariff), which may, if persistently underfilled, constitute a disguised restriction to trade. Finally, ministers restated an agreement reached in 2005 in Hong Kong to eliminate all export subsidies (the original target date was 2013). This goal will now be part of the final Doha agreement. Ministers also agreed to an examination process to enhance transparency and monitoring of export subsidies. Thus, fostering competition in international agricultural trade remains a priority for the post-Bali work programme. In other words, the envisaged examination process on export subsidies and equivalent measures would be harnessed to support reform (see below on the extent of agricultural protection in developed countries).

The third part of the Bali Package deals with issues specific to LDCs, a continuing theme at WTO (table 1). Negotiations leading up to Bali were based on a proposal from the LDC group encompassing: (i) the operationalization of LDC services waivers; (ii) the expansion of coverage of duty-free and quota-free (DFQF) access; (iii) preferential rules of origin; and (iv) a decision on cotton.

...as were concerns of LDCs

The 2011 WTO ministerial meeting had agreed to permit fifteen-year waivers from most-favoured-nation (MFN) treatment to allow preferential access for LDC services exports, as had already been allowed for goods.[7] These waivers, however, did not confer any automatic economic benefit. They had to be applied in ways that helped create the conditions under which firms in LDCs could export services to a preference-granting country. None had been approved prior to the Bali meeting. The operationalization of the services waiver decision at Bali is aimed at helping LDCs secure meaningful preferences for their services and service suppliers. The LDCs are to submit a collective request regarding the sectors that are of export interest to them in which they would like to have preferential market access. A high-level meeting will then be convened to respond to this request. This could amount to a significant effort to identify commercially meaningful ways to operationalize the waiver to facilitate exports of services from countries most in need.[8] Therefore, LDCs need to be assisted in preparing this request. However, the potential value of the waiver to LDCs appears to be rather limited, unless preferential access includes the supply of services categorized under Mode 4, that is, cross-border provision of services by natural persons.

The Bali Ministerial Declaration and decisions reaffirmed—albeit in non-binding language—the targets of the 2005 Hong Kong Declaration of providing DFQF access to products exported from LDCs, and encouraged, in particular, developed-country WTO members to improve existing DFQF product and coun-

---

7 World Trade Organization, "WTO ministers adopt waiver to permit preferential treatment of LDC service suppliers", 17 December 2011, available from http://www.wto.org/english/news_e/news11_e/serv_17dec11_e.htm.

8 Sherry Stephenson and Anne-Katrin Pfister, "The LDC services waiver beyond Bali", *Bridges Africa*, vol. 2, No. 8 (15 November 2013).

try coverage. Research suggests that achieving the Doha objective of full DFQF coverage remains a valuable goal for the LDC group. This is because the exclusion of even a relatively small number of products has an impact in terms of LDC exports, owing to the concentration of individual LDCs in a narrow range of products.[9]

Table 1

Doha Round milestones in addressing the issues of least developed countries (LDCs)

2002	Members adopt guidelines to help facilitate WTO accession negotiations for LDCs
2005	Ministers in Hong Kong SAR[a] adopt decision-setting goal to provide DFQF market access on a lasting basis for all products originating from LDCs. Members also agree to eliminate cotton export subsidies, and that developed countries would allow cotton from LDCs into their markets on a DFQF basis
December 2011	The Council for Trade-related Aspects of Intellectual Property (TRIPS) is instructed to consider requests by LDCs for extension of the transition period to come into compliance with the TRIPS Agreement. WTO ministers adopt waiver that would allow members to grant preferential treatment to services and service suppliers from LDCs
July 2012	WTO General Council formally signs off on revised LDC accession guidelines, aimed at further strengthening, streamlining and operationalizing the 2002 guidelines on accession to WTO
May 2013	LDC group submits communication highlighting its priority issues for the Bali Ministerial Conference
June 2013	WTO members agree to extend TRIPS transition period for LDCs until July 2021
Fall 2013	Convergence deemed close for some LDC draft decisions for Bali Ministerial Conference. Subsequent impasse in Geneva process puts full Bali Package in question
December 2013	Bali Ministerial Conference adopts package including LDC measures

Source: Adapted from International Centre for Trade and Sustainable Development, "A Brief Guide to Negotiations at the WTO's Ninth Ministerial Conference", 2013.
a Special Administrative Region.

The Ministerial Decision on rules of origin in Bali set voluntary guidelines to make them more flexible, more transparent and simpler in determining eligibility for preferential access of imports from LDCs. The guidelines will allow LDC exporters to use foreign inputs—up to a maximum of 75 per cent of the final value of the good—for goods to qualify under LDC preferential trade arrangements, as well as treat inputs from other LDCs and the developed-country importer as though they were local content. The guidelines represent a useful step towards the harmonization of preferential rules of origin globally. Nonetheless, they remain a set of voluntary disciplines and thus subject to the good will of each preference-granting country, although such guidelines should be followed in the design of unilateral preference schemes or new preferential schemes.[10]

The Bali Declaration also reaffirmed the 2005 Hong Kong mandate underlining the importance of effective assistance to the cotton sector (as delivered through the Aid for Trade and the Enhanced Integrated Framework initiatives),

---

9 For example, recent simulations of different scenarios under the African Growth and Opportunity Act of the United States for post-2015 show that extending preferential treatment to the 1 per cent most sensitive products would potentially entail the most significant benefits for eligible African countries (Simon Mevel and others, *The African Growth and Opportunity Act: An Empirical Analysis of the Possibilities Post-2015* (Washington, D.C.: African Growth Initiative at Brookings; and Addis Ababa: United Nations Economic Commission for Africa, July 2013).

10 United Nations Economic Commission for Africa, "From Doha to Bali: the unfinished business and the lessons for Africa", mimeo, April 2014.

and enhanced transparency and monitoring of the trade-related aspects of cotton policies. Members also agreed "to hold a dedicated discussion on a biannual basis in the Committee on Agriculture in special session to examine relevant trade-related developments across the three pillars of market access, domestic support and export competition in relation to cotton".[11] This will provide an entry point for the Cotton-4 countries (Benin, Burkina Faso, Chad and Mali) to advance their concerns in the future. There has been no progress, however, on elimination of cotton subsidies.

WTO members have long sought to review the agreement to accord "special and differential treatment" (SDT) to developing countries in trade negotiations "with a view to strengthening [the provisions] and making them more precise, effective and operational", as per paragraph 44 of the Doha Declaration. In Bali, a decision was taken to set up a Monitoring Mechanism for SDT, with a circumscribed mandate that the outcome of the review shall not alter or affect members' rights and obligations. Following the review of a provision, the monitoring mechanism may make a recommendation to the relevant WTO body to initiate negotiations on the provisions reviewed; this recommendation will "inform the work of the relevant body, but not define or limit its final determination".[12]

> A mechanism to monitor special and differential treatment is to be implemented

Next steps for multilateral trade negotiations

The agreement reached in Bali encompasses a limited and least controversial subset of the issues of the Doha Round. WTO ministers were instructed to prepare, by December 2014, a clearly defined work programme to conclude the Doha Round. There is recognition that tough issues lie ahead, particularly concerning industrial goods, services and agriculture—so crucial for many developing countries.[13]

What the Bali Package will mean in terms of enhancing global economic integration and whether it will breathe new life into the multilateral trade talks remains to be seen. The list of unresolved issues contains many possible stumbling blocks. Even decisions in the Package that are binding will require time and commitment from the parties in order to have a positive effect on international trade.

Several alternative scenarios are usually put forward when discussing the future of the Doha Round and the WTO in general. One scenario is to conclude a "Doha light"[14] agreement featuring less contested items. However, this means that important trade policy issues, particularly those that are important to developing countries, such as agricultural subsidies, might not be addressed. A second scenario involves concluding a number of "mini" packages such as the Bali Package. The upside to this approach is that it helps create momentum, and also helps ensure that progress in some areas is not blocked by an impasse in others. The risk is that issues that are important to developing countries might not be dealt with in the immediate future. Additional countries could join the agreements ex

> Four scenarios are possible going forward

---

11 World Trade Organization Draft Ministerial Decision on Cotton, WT/MIN(13)/W/13, 6 December 2013, para. 5.

12 World Trade Organization Draft Ministerial Decision on the Monitoring Mechanism on Special and Differential Treatment, WT/MIN(13)/W/17, 5 December 2013, para. 7.

13 World Trade Organization, "Azevêdo to push for trade role in future sustainable development goals", 5 May 2014.

14 This term is used to refer to the Bali Package and to the possibility of reducing the Doha agenda in order to be able to conclude a less ambitious agreement.

post, but would be accepting the adopted terms rather than participating in their negotiation. The third scenario, a new deadlock, is, of course, the least favourable. Finally, the scenario that would be most favourable to developing countries, and the multilateral trading system, would be a conclusion of the Round that adheres to its single undertaking and ensures that all areas of the negotiations have an outcome consistent with the mandate provided at Doha.

Other trade policy developments

Trade-restrictive measures increased in 2013

Members of the Group of Twenty (G20), at the September 2013 Saint Petersburg Summit, extended their commitment to refrain from protectionist measures that they had made at the onset of the global economic and financial crisis.[15] However, recent WTO monitoring reports[16] show that the number of new trade restrictions increased between mid-May and mid-November 2013, with most G20 members having put in place new trade restrictions or measures that have the potential to limit trade; 116 new trade-restrictive measures have been identified since the last WTO report, up from 109 measures recorded for the previous seven-month period.[17] While these new measures affect about only 1.1 per cent of G20 merchandise imports, the G20 needs to fully implement its anti-protectionism commitment to maintain confidence in its parallel commitment to an open and liberal trading system.

Protectionism of environmental goods is a concern

The multilateral trading system supports the right of WTO members to take measures to advance legitimate goals such as protection of the environment, while ensuring such measures are not applied arbitrarily and are not disguised protectionism (box 1). But the increasing use of trade remedies and litigation related to the application of environmental policies raises questions about appropriate multilateral policies, including possible changes to WTO agreements to accommodate the need to support sustainable development goals. This is a potential focus for future WTO consideration, given concerns that these measures may lead to hidden protectionism.

Box 1

Green industrial policy, trade remedies and litigation

a Mark Wu and James Salzman, "The next generation of trade and environment conflicts: the rise of green industrial policy", draft paper, April 2013.

Interest in the interface between trade and environment policy heightened in the 1990s. Members of the recently established WTO brought cases to its dispute settlement mechanism to challenge policies that had been adopted by trading partners under the guise of environmental protection, but that seemed protectionist in intent. The tuna/dolphin, turtle/shrimp and United States gasoline cases were emblematic of this first wave of trade and environment conflicts. In these early cases, the importing countries—mostly developed countries—imposed market access restrictions on goods from third countries with a view to promoting improvements in environmental behaviour.[a]

---

15 See G20 Leaders' Declaration, Saint Petersburg Summit, 5 and 6 September 2013, available from https://www.g20.org/sites/default/files/g20_resources/library/Saint_Petersburg_Declaration_ENG_0.pdf.

16 World Trade Organization, "Report on G-20 Trade Measures (mid-May 2013 to mid-November 2013)", 18 December 2013.

17 These were mainly new trade remedy actions, in particular the initiation of anti-dumping investigations, tariff increases and more stringent customs procedures.

Similar policy concerns have been raised regarding the potential use of unilateral border measures by importing countries who undertake climate change mitigation measures that raise domestic production costs relative to those of non-participating exporters. The intention of the border measures is to raise the prices of import competitors or spur climate action by exporting countries. The confluence of environment and industrial policy considerations has had its starkest manifestation in the renewable energy sector where developed and developing countries alike have taken action to encourage the adoption of renewable energy through a policy mix, including consumption targets, subsidies, loans and tax credits, local content requirements, and feed-in tariffs (FITs), which promote investment in the production of renewable energy sources. But trading partners have resorted to trade rules that challenge the use of particular policies and/or address their negative effects on trade, employment and industrial development.

b Cathleen Cimino and Gary Hufbauer, "Trade remedies targeting the renewable energy sector", report prepared for the United Nations Conference on Trade and Development Ad Hoc Expert Group Meeting on Trade and Environment, April 2014, p. 12.

In this context, analysts have highlighted the significant increase of anti-dumping (AD) and countervailing duties (CVD) in the renewable energy sector. According to a recent study, "some 41 AD and CVD cases have been initiated since 2008 on biofuels, solar energy and wind energy products. Notably, almost half of these measures target solar energy products. The trade remedy trend accelerated during the period 2012–2013 among major producers of renewable energy, including Australia, China, the European Union (EU), India and the United States".[b] The same study estimates the value of trade lost as a consequence of trade remedy actions at $68 billion over a five-year period.

WTO members have also used the dispute settlement mechanism to challenge green policies of trading partners, including the following: export restrictions by China on raw materials brought by the EU, Mexico and the United States in 2009, and export restrictions on rare earth minerals imposed by China (questioned by the EU, Japan and the United States in 2012); local content requirements established by China to qualify for subsidies on wind power equipment, challenged by the United States in 2011; local content requirement of the FIT established by Canada, challenged by the EU and Japan in 2011; local content restrictions in the European FITs, challenged by China in 2012; and the case brought against India's FIT programme in 2013 by the United States. In most of the adjudicated cases, the decisions have favoured the complaining party.[c]

c See Mark Wu and James Salzman, op. cit.

Trade policy implementation

Preferential access and tariff barriers

After the completion of the Uruguay Round in 1994, tariffs fell to zero on a substantial number of products, partly owing to the fact that a large proportion of the duty-free imports (80 per cent) had resulted from the multilateral elimination of tariffs under the MFN. Additional preferences are given to LDCs. Access to LDC products in developed markets has been defined by two main trends. First, all developing countries receive increased duty-free treatment to their exports. Second, LDCs increased their exports of dutiable textile and agricultural products where they had a competitive advantage. An increasing share of these dutiable products has been gradually incorporated into duty-free schemes. Hence, duty-free access for LDCs has always been higher than for developing countries as a whole (figure 1). Unlike other developing countries, most of the duty-free treatment granted to LDCs is truly preferential (i.e., not MFN treatment).

Figure 1

Proportion of developed-country imports from developing countries admitted duty free, 2000–2012 (*percentage*)

Developing countries,
excluding arms

LDCs, excluding arms

Developing countries,
excluding arms and oil

LDCs, excluding
arms and oil

Source: ITC/UNCTAD/WTO
database.

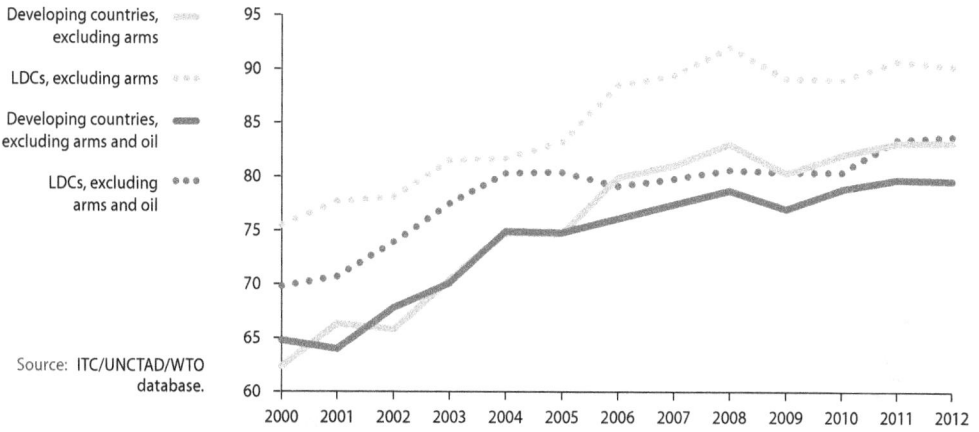

Agricultural exports from
LDCs receive the largest
preference

During the decade after the end of the Uruguay Round, the average tariff applied by developed countries to textile and clothing products from developing countries decreased by 2 and 3 percentage points, respectively, but by only 1 percentage point for agricultural products. From 2005 to 2012, there was an additional point reduction in tariffs applied to agricultural products, but a less significant tariff reduction has been observed for textiles and clothing (figure 2). LDC exports faced similar conditions in terms of tariff reductions, but the difference in the treatment of agricultural products from 2005 onwards was more marked (figure 3). This is partly explained by the fact that many developed countries already provided comprehensive duty-free treatment to the other categories of products. LDC agricultural exports to developed-country markets have continued to receive increasing preferences. In fact, LDC agricultural exports receive the largest preference margin relative to competing products from other developing countries.

Figure 2

Average tariffs imposed by developed countries on key products from developing countries, 1996–2012, selected years (*percentage ad valorem*)

2012
2005
2000
1996

Source: ITC/UNCTAD/WTO
database.

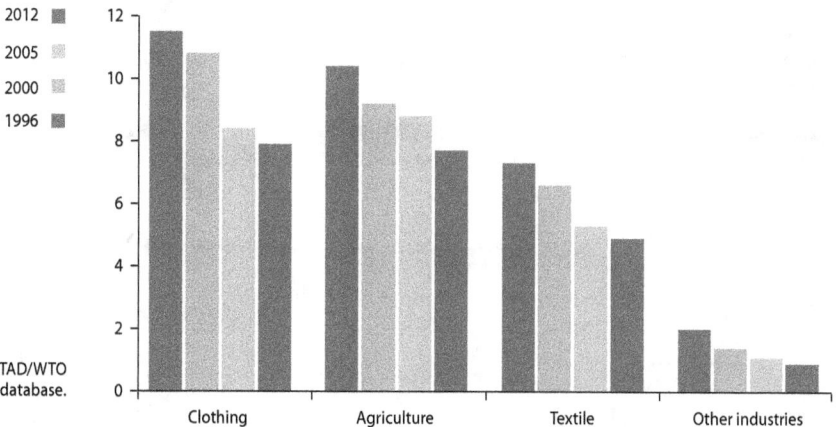

Figure 3

Average tariffs imposed by developed countries on key products from least developed countries, 1996–2012, selected years (*percentage ad valorem*)

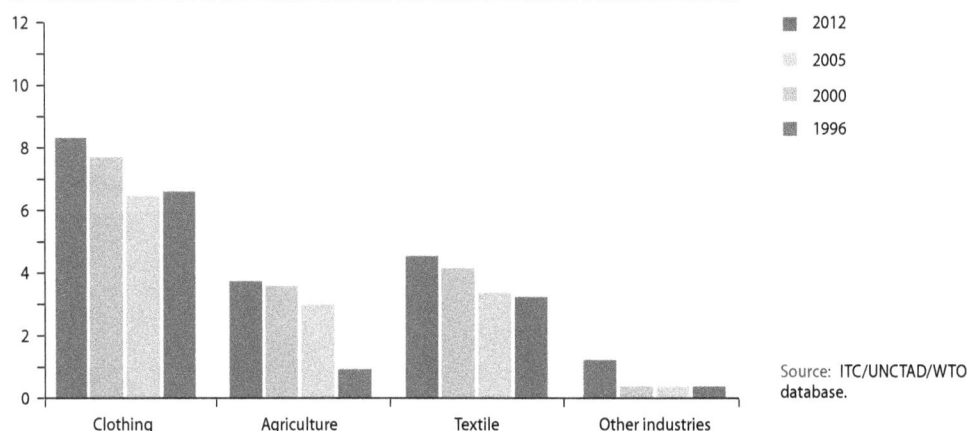

Legend:
- 2012
- 2005
- 2000
- 1996

Source: ITC/UNCTAD/WTO database.

Tariff peaks and tariff escalation

The structure of tariff schemes and their different rates across different imported products also matter for determining the degree of market access. Tariff peaks refer to a situation where tariffs on some products are considerably higher than usual, defined as above 15 per cent. As shown in table 2, over 9 per cent of tariff lines continue to be affected by tariff peaks in high-income member countries of the Organization for Economic Cooperation and Development (OECD), with little change over the past decade. Tariff peaks affect mainly agricultural products, which remain at 36 per cent of tariff lines.

Another negative aspect of tariff schemes is tariff escalation, wherein a country applies a higher tariff rate to products at the later stages of production. Thus, tariff escalation gives relatively stronger protection to products in the same category with more value added. The degree of tariff escalation for agricultural products increased in 2013, with the difference between tariffs applied on processed agricultural products and those for raw agricultural products remaining high.

Tariff escalation for agricultural products increased

Table 2

Tariff peaks and escalation in high-income OECD countries, 2000 and 2007–2013 (*percentage*)[a]

	2000	2007	2008	2009	2010	2011	2012	2013
Tariff peaks[b]								
All goods	9.2	9.3	9.0	8.9	8.8	9.3	9.7	9.6
Agricultural	33.4	37.4	37.5	36.5	34.6	36.3	36.0	35.8
Non-agricultural	3.1	2.2	2.2	2.2	2.2	2.3	2.5	2.6
Tariff escalation[c]								
All goods	1.0	0.1	0.1	0.1	0.1	0.2	-0.4	-0.1
Agricultural	12.6	11.2	11.8	11.2	9.8	11.2	10.0	10.5
Non-agricultural	2.1	1.3	1.4	1.4	1.2	1.2	0.3	0.3

Source: ITC.
a Values shown are averages weighted by share in world imports.
b Proportion of total tariff lines in a country's MFN tariff schedule with tariffs above 15 per cent.
c Percentage point difference between the applied tariffs for finished (fully processed) goods and the applied tariffs for raw materials. Prior to aggregation over countries, the country average is a simple average of Harmonized System, six-digit duty averages.

Agricultural subsidies in OECD countries

OECD countries alone spent $258 billion in subsidies to support farmers in their respective countries in 2013 (table 3). As a percentage of farm receipts, support changed little in 2013 and, overall, remained lower than in recent years. The part of this support that is directly linked to production—the most trade-distorting type—still represents about half of the total. Recent developments on subsidies policy include the new five-year Farm Bill signed into law in February 2014 in the United States of America. The new law reaffirms the United States Government's longstanding support to farmers through 2018.

Table 3

Source: OECD, "Producer and Consumer Support Estimates", OECD Agriculture statistics (database), 2014.
a Preliminary data.
b The General Services Support Estimate (GSSE) indicator has been calculated using a revised methodology. As the GSSE is a component of the Total Support Estimate (TSE), both GSSE and TSE data series have been revised. The revised GSSE is defined as "budgetary expenditure that creates enabling conditions for the primary agricultural sector through development of private or public services, institutions and infrastructure". This definition replaces the previous, broader, definition of the GSSE as "payments to eligible private or public services provided to agriculture generally".

Agricultural support in OECD countries, 1990, 2000 and 2007–2013

	1990	2000	2007	2008	2009	2010	2011	2012	2013[a]
Total agricultural support in OECD countries[b]									
In billions of United States dollars	311	304	314	342	326	328	342	350	344
In billions of euros	245	329	229	234	235	248	246	273	259
As a percentage of OECD countries' GDP	2.27	1.07	0.79	0.83	0.82	0.79	0.79	0.79	0.75
Support to agricultural producers in OECD countries									
In billions of United States dollars	251.1	245.0	243.8	261.0	247.9	245.9	258.5	266.4	258.0
In billions of euros	197.8	265.9	178.1	178.5	178.5	185.7	185.9	207.2	194.3
As a percentage of gross farm receipts (percentage PSE)	31.8	32.3	20.8	20.4	21.8	19.5	18.2	18.8	18.2

Aid for Trade

Aid for Trade increased in 2012

Donor countries and institutions have continued to support developing-country efforts to build trade capacity through initiatives such as Aid for Trade and the Enhanced Integrated Framework for Trade-related Assistance for LDCs. Following a decline in 2011, Aid for Trade grew again in 2012 (data are unavailable for 2013). This increase was driven by aid to economic infrastructure, which expanded by 31 per cent, to almost $31 billion, accounting for 57 per cent of total flows, a slightly higher share than in previous years. Most of the increase in Aid for Trade was allocated to middle-income countries (MICs), which received $31 billion (or 58 per cent of the total), a growth of 38 per cent from 2011. In contrast, LDCs received $13.1 billion (or 24 per cent of the total), down 2 per cent from 2011, mainly driven by reduced support in post-war efforts in Afghanistan (figure 4). The growth rate of disbursements slowed to 6 per cent in 2012 from an average of over 10 per cent during 2010 and 2011.

A hardening of the terms of Aid for Trade was also evident. While traditionally there had been an even split between concessional loans and grants, in 2011 and 2012 loans assumed greater prominence, such that in 2012 almost 65 per cent of Aid for Trade was provided as loans. A majority of the funds committed to the LDCs, however, remained in the form of grants.

Figure 4
Aid for Trade commitments by income group, 2002–2012 (*billions of 2012 dollars*)

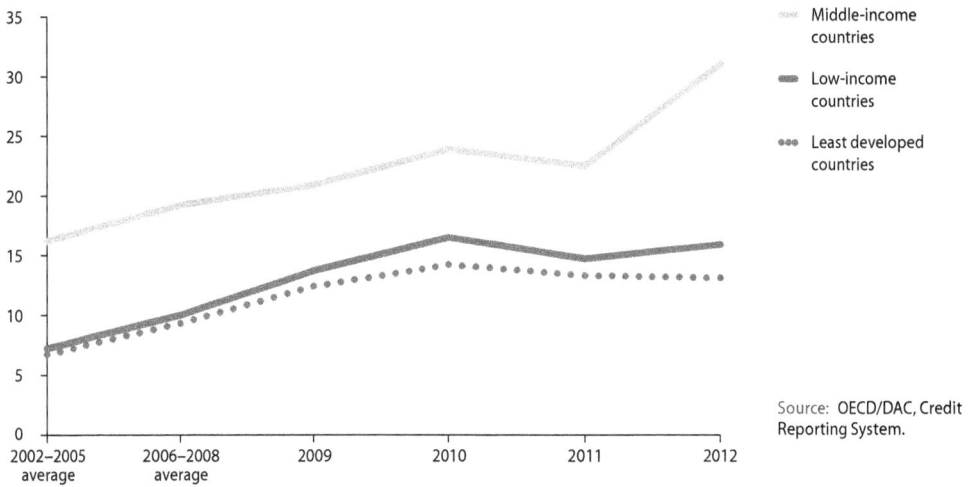

Middle-income
countries

Low-income
countries

Least developed
countries

Source: OECD/DAC, Credit
Reporting System.

Growth in flows reflected increasing support for road building, particularly in Africa, and electricity-generation projects. Aid for building productive capacity continued to expand, rising 10 per cent to a new high of $21.6 billion. These resources have helped support agricultural development, investments in banking and finance institutions and private-sector development programmes. On the other hand, aid for strengthening trade policy and regulations has not grown since 2009 and has stagnated at $1.3 billion (figure 5), even as assistance for trade facilitation has increased.

Figure 5
Aid for Trade commitments by category, 2002–2012 (*billions of 2012 dollars*)

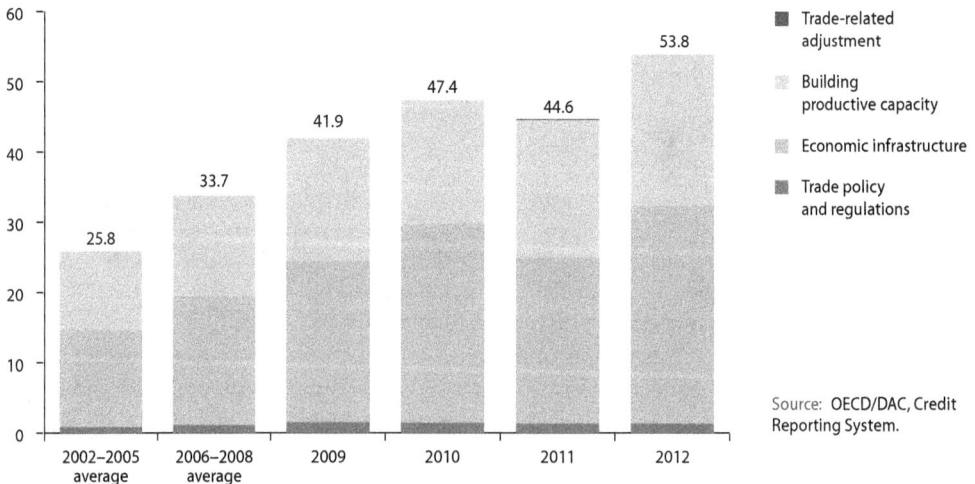

Trade-related
adjustment

Building
productive capacity

Economic infrastructure

Trade policy
and regulations

Source: OECD/DAC, Credit
Reporting System.

The scaling up of Aid for Trade commitments since 2006 has largely ben-efited Africa, whose share over the course of the base period 2002–2005 was 30 per cent, rising to 40 per cent in 2012. The continent received $21 billion in 2012 (figure 6), with most of this increase concentrated in transportation (roads and rails, including improving roads between Mombasa, Nairobi and Addis Ababa), electrical transmission and agriculture. The largest recipients were Kenya ($2.3 billion), Morocco ($2.3 billion), Egypt ($2.1 billion) and Ethiopia ($2 billion). Support to the Americas and Asia also improved moderately over 2011 levels. However, Asia's share of total Aid for Trade has fluctuated: while it received almost half of total Aid for Trade in 2002–2005, its share declined over time to 33 per cent in 2012. In 2011 and 2012, commitments to Europe increased, mostly owing to greater Aid for Trade in Turkey and Serbia and increasing loans to the region by the European Union (EU).

Figure 6

Aid for Trade commitments by region, 2002–2005 and 2010–2012

(*billions of 2012 dollars*)

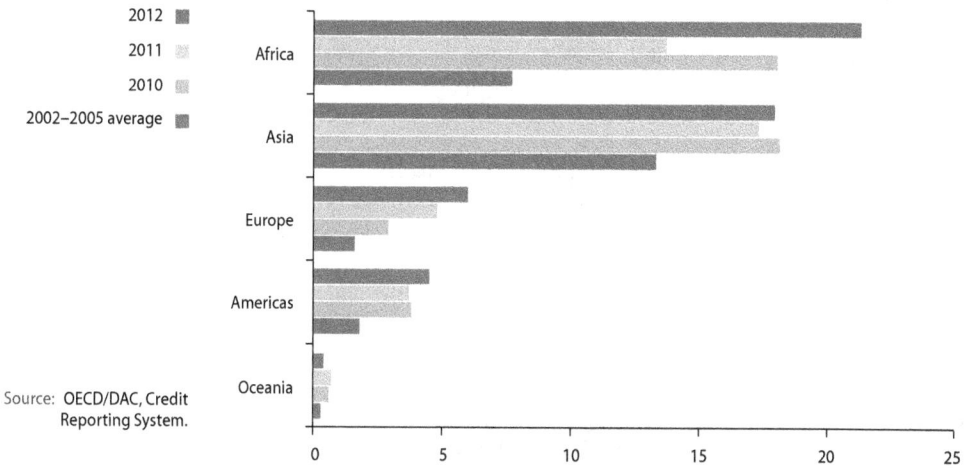

Source: OECD/DAC, Credit Reporting System.

Policy issues for the future

Trade in services is growing in importance

A number of increasingly salient policy concerns may (and should) impact the trade policy agenda going forward. Trade in services, for example, plays a critical role in global trade and continues to grow in importance. Modern communications has enabled significant growth in international trade in services. More so than for trade in goods, international trade in services is dominated by developed countries. LDC services trade, in particular, is marginal, accounting for about 0.6 per cent of global exports of services and 1.7 per cent of imports.[18] With the Bali Package agreement on operationalizing the services waiver, as discussed above, the opportunity for boosting developing-country services exports is growing.

18 World Trade Organization, "Participation of developing economies in the global trad-ing system", note by the Secretariat, Committee on Trade and Development, 14 Octo-ber 2013 (WT/COMTD/W/201).

However, compared to the vast literature on policies affecting trade in goods, the empirical analysis of services trade policy is still in its infancy, which is hindering policy development. A major constraint has been inadequate data on policies affecting services trade, especially in developing countries.[19] Across regions, some of the fastest growing countries in Asia and the Gulf States have the most restrictive policies in services, whereas some other developing countries, including Cambodia, Ghana, Mongolia and Senegal are remarkably open. While most OECD countries are generally quite open overall, they tend to exhibit greater restrictiveness in transportation services and limit the movement of natural persons as service suppliers. In fact, across sectors, professional and transportation services are among the most protected in both industrial and developing countries, while retail, telecommunications and even finance tend to be more open.

Policymakers have also begun to focus more attention on global value chains (GVCs), in which the value added in the various steps in commercial product development—from conception to design to collection of raw material inputs to large-scale production, marketing and distribution—may each take place in different countries around the world. The rapid expansion of GVCs has opened new trade opportunities for several developing countries. For the majority of smaller developing economies with limited natural resource endowments, there is often considerable interest in developing strategies that incorporate greater participation in GVCs.[20] Joining value chains and upgrading domestic firms' participation require designing and implementing strategies that tackle barriers to integration.

Global value chains are expanding…

Among the main obstacles that LDC firms, in particular, face in expanding their participation in value chains is inadequate domestic infrastructure, cumbersome customs procedures, lack of access to trade finance, high trade transaction costs and failure to comply with sanitary and phytosanitary requirements or technical standards of importing countries.[21] Other factors that drive up production and trading costs and undermine competitiveness in LDCs include low stocks of skilled labour and the disadvantages of geography (such as inadequate natural harbours). This translates into a substantial disadvantage in nurturing exporters that can attain the scale and reliable quality necessary to be competitive in global markets.[22] Evidence shows that supply chains tend to go where the logistics are smooth and uncertainty is low. Many of the poorest developing countries remain unprepared to benefit from the networks of GVCs and thus often remain dependent on a few primary commodity exports. Aid for Trade can play an increasingly important role in this regard.

…but LDCs are facing challenges

---

19 Ingo Borchert, Batshur Gootiiz and Aaditya Mattoo, "Policy barriers to international trade in services: evidence from a new database", World Bank Policy Research Working Paper, WPS6109, June 2012.

20 United Nations Conference on Trade and Development, *World Investment Report 2013: Global Value Chains: Investment and Trade for Development*, Sales No. E.13.II.D.5.

21 Hubert Escaith and Bekele Tamenu, "Least-developed countries' trade during the 'super-cycle' and the great trade collapse: patterns and stylized facts", World Trade Organization Staff Working Paper, ERSD-2013–12, 27 November 2013; and Economic Commission for Africa, *Building Trade Capacities for Africa's Transformation: A Critical Review of Aid for Trade*, Addis Ababa, 2013.

22 International Trade Centre, *LDCs and Global Value Chains: Using Aid for Trade to Seize New Opportunities*, Geneva, November 2013.

It is also appropriate to consider new targets for international trade policy liberalization in the post-2015 era. Because developed countries have lowered the majority of their tariffs, the potential for further improvement in market access from further tariff reduction is limited, notwithstanding the tariff peaks and tariff escalation remaining in various products of export interest to developing countries. However, there is considerable scope for action on non-tariff measures that limit market access in both developed and developing countries. Also, because the main source of growth in world trade today is South-South trade, additional focus on further reducing barriers to this trade may be warranted—through greater development of trade preference schemes granted by emerging and middle-income developing countries to LDCs, for example, as well as through deepening regional trade integration.

With regard to national trade policy priorities, setting and implementing meaningful trade diversification targets can help increase the resilience to economic shocks, for low-income countries in particular. Attention should also be paid to the gender impact of the expansion of various export- and import-competing sectors. The right mix of trade, investment, environment and other policy measures can help optimize the impact of trade as an enabler for environmental sustainability and poverty reduction.

In sum, looking at the current international trade policy landscape, the question arises whether the Doha Round still covers the most pertinent trade issues or whether the multilateral trade agenda needs a fundamental revision. This question relates both to content and the decision-making process. The Doha trade talks started more than a decade ago and the international trade and political order has since changed considerably. The number of bilateral and regional trade agreements has increased substantially in the past decade and will probably continue. Some of the multi-country agreements currently under negotiation, such as the Trans-Pacific Partnership and the Transatlantic Trade and Investment Partnership, might have a major impact on international trade. There is no guarantee that developing-country considerations will be taken into account in those negotiations. WTO was created to be the global forum for creating the open, multilateral trading system to which the international community aspired and still aspires. Bali breathed new energy into the role of the WTO as a forum for negotiations, but also reinforced views on the difficulty in achieving ambitious reforms at the multilateral level. This poses a challenge to the entire multilateral approach to development cooperation, which the international community must address.

Policy Recommendations

As the deadline for achieving the MDGs fast approaches, accelerated efforts by the international community will be required. Actions required at the national and international levels to ensure and further improve market access for developing countries include the following:

- WTO members should give priority to ambitious negotiation outcomes, particularly those on agriculture, in the post-Bali work programme, with a view to reaching a balanced conclusion of the Doha Round of trade negotiations
- All countries should remove trade-restrictive measures adopted since the onset of the global crisis and avoid the introduction of new ones
- WTO members should effectively implement the Bali Package, with particular emphasis on the Trade Facilitation Agreement and the operationalization of the LDC package of measures
- Developed countries should eliminate all forms of agricultural export subsidies and trade-distorting domestic support
- Developed countries should increase support for capacity-building in developing countries, including capacity to meet meaningful trade diversification targets and to comply with international standards and non-tariff measures through, inter alia, sustainable and predictable Aid for Trade and the Enhanced Integrated Framework for LDCs

Debt sustainability

Since the United Nations Millennium Summit in 2000, there has been considerable change in the landscape of sovereign debt in developing countries, with many low- and middle-income countries accessing international capital markets, some of them for the first time. The debt indicators of Goal 8 of the Millennium Development Goals (MDGs) focused on the debt difficulties of the heavily indebted poor countries (HIPCs), which have largely been addressed under the terms of the HIPC Initiative and the Multilateral Debt Relief Initiative (MDRI) that complemented it. This is not to say that there are no new risks in some of the HIPC countries, or that other low- or middle-income countries have not also faced debt crises since 2000. In particular, as discussed below, there is currently reason for concern about the debt situation of a number of small States. While Goal 8 contained no indicators for addressing debt crises in non-HIPCs, it implicitly addressed these countries when it called for policies that would lead to sustainable debt levels for all developing countries.

Progress under the HIPC Initiative and MDRI

The HIPC Initiative is drawing to a close, with 35 out of 39 eligible countries reaching the completion point as of March 2014 (table 1).[1] Chad remains the only country in the interim phase, where it receives temporary relief. The three currently eligible countries—Eritrea, Somalia and the Sudan—have yet to start the process of qualifying for debt relief under the Initiative, although the Sudan has taken a first step. The Government of the Sudan has agreed on a new Staff-Monitored Program (SMP) with the International Monetary Fund (IMF) for 2014, which is a step towards building the track record of sound policies required for HIPC relief.[2] Three additional countries— Myanmar, Nepal and Zimbabwe—are deemed potentially eligible for the Initiative, but international decisions on their eligibility are still pending. Nevertheless, on the positive side, in January 2013 the Paris Club of bilateral official creditors cleared Myanmar's $10 billion[3] of arrears, of which $5.5 billion were cancelled and the rest rescheduled.[4] Otherwise, the HIPC Initiative has now been closed.

Debt-relief programmes are coming to an end...

---

1 Information in this section is largely drawn from International Monetary Fund, "Debt relief under the Heavily Indebted Poor Countries (HIPC) Initiative", IMF Fact Sheet, March 2014, available from http://www.imf.org/external/np/exr/facts/hipc.htm; and "Heavily Indebted Poor Countries (HIPC) Initiative and Multilateral Debt Relief Initiative (MDRI)—Statistical update", December 2013, available from https://www.imf.org/external/np/pp/eng/2013/121913.pdf.

2 "IMF Managing Director approves new Staff-Monitored Program for Sudan", IMF press release No. 14/139, 27 March 2014.

3 All monetary amounts are expressed in United Stated dollars, except where otherwise indicated.

4 "The Paris Club and the Republic of the Union of Myanmar agree on a cancellation of USD 5 925 million", Paris Club press release, 28 January 2013, available from http://

Table 1

Debt-relief status of HIPCs (*at end-March 2014*)

35 post-completion-point HIPCs[a]				
Afghanistan	Comoros	Guinea	Malawi	Sao Tome and Principe
Benin	Congo	Guinea-Bissau	Mali	Senegal
Bolivia	Côte d'Ivoire	Guyana	Mauritania	Sierra Leone
Burkina Faso	Democratic Republic of the Congo	Haiti	Mozambique	Togo
Burundi	Ethiopia	Honduras	Nicaragua	Uganda
Cameroon	Gambia	Liberia	Niger	United Republic of Tanzania
Central African Republic	Ghana	Madagascar	Rwanda	Zambia
1 interim HIPC[b]				
Chad				
3 pre-decision-point HIPCs[c]				
Eritrea		Somalia		Sudan

Source: World Bank, HIPC/
MDRI Update, March 2014.
a Countries that have qualified
for irrevocable debt relief
under the HIPC Initiative.
b Countries that have reached
the decision point under the
HIPC Initiative, but have not
yet reached the completion
point.
c Countries that are eligible
or potentially eligible and may
wish to avail themselves of the
HIPC Initiative or the MDRI.

Debt relief under the HIPC and MDRI initiatives has substantially alleviated debt burdens in assisted countries and has facilitated their efforts to increase
poverty-reducing expenditures. In 2013, debt service of the HIPCs was, on average, 1.6 per cent of gross domestic product (GDP), while poverty-reducing expenditures were more than 10.0 per cent of GDP.[5] While the latter has been higher
than the former at least since the Millennium Declaration, the difference has
risen from an estimated 3.7 percentage points in 2001 to almost 9.0 percentage
points in 2013, as the debt-servicing ratio declined.

...but some assisted
countries are at risk of debt
distress

Nevertheless, having borrowed from various official and private external
sources since receiving relief, several HIPCs are again at high or moderate risk
of renewed debt distress. This underscores the need to sufficiently increase grant
resources for the world's poorest countries.

The official creditors that cancelled repayment obligations of HIPCs
incurred costs in the sense that they abandoned claims for repayment and these
claims had to be covered from other creditor resources. The present value (PV) as
at end-2012 of total HIPC relief thus far extended is estimated at $74.3 billion,
while the 2012 PV of the MDRI for the four participating multilateral creditors
(IMF, World Bank, African Development Bank and Inter-American Development Bank) is estimated at $39.7 billion. Paris Club creditors have committed
to providing debt relief estimated at $21.3 billion in 2012 PV terms to the 36
countries that have reached decision points. Most members of the Paris Club
have also voluntarily committed to providing additional debt relief beyond that
required under the HIPC Initiative.

www.clubdeparis.org/sections/communication/communiques/myanmar-20130128/
viewLanguage/en.
5 International Monetary Fund, "Heavily Indebted Poor Countries (HIPC) Initiative and
Multilateral Debt Relief Initiative (MDRI)—Statistical update", op. cit.

Non-Paris Club bilateral creditors, as a whole, have delivered about 47 per cent of their share of HIPC Initiative debt relief; however, about one third of such creditors have not yet delivered any.[6] And while there has been some increase in delivery over the past few years, the rate of delivery remains low and participation from these creditor groups needs to be strengthened.

Moreover, some commercial creditors continue to litigate to recover the full face value of their loans, plus interest and penalties in many cases. In 2013, the World Bank and IMF reported that litigation was ongoing against eight HIPCs. Such legal struggles not only have adverse financial consequences for the poorest countries, but also take up considerable time and resources of debtor-government authorities.

The debt situation in developing countries

On average, the debt situation of developing countries seems generally benign. The difficulty, of course, is that the more worrisome cases are hidden by the aggregated data. In this context, it is useful to view not only the debt situation of developing countries as a whole but also the situation of a group of small States, where a number of countries have been caught in debt difficulties (box 1). However, there is also an emerging vulnerability in developing countries that may be seen in part in the aggregate data.

The overall picture of the debt situation hides some vulnerabilities such as...

In aggregate, the external debt of the developing countries measured only 22.6 per cent of their GDP. This compares to 33.5 per cent of GDP a decade earlier. As may be seen in figure 1, there had been a relatively widespread decline in the debt ratios of the three groupings of developing countries until the onset of the global financial crisis in 2007–2008, when the debt ratios of low-income and lower-middle-income countries rose in response. Only the upper-middle-income countries, which are less dependent on external sources of funding, maintained their external debt-to-GDP ratios, albeit no longer reducing them further.

Box 1
Debt difficulties in small States[a]

Many small States present special—and in some cases long-standing—debt sustainability challenges. In 2013, the average ratio of public debt to GDP of small States amounted to 107.7 per cent, while their ratio of external debt to GDP averaged 57.7 per cent. In contrast, the total public debt of developing countries as a whole was only 26.4 per cent of GDP (see figure). Moreover, the International Monetary Fund (IMF) estimated that to prevent the debt-to-GDP ratios of small States from rising further, about half of the small States in a sample it studied would require some additional degree of fiscal consolidation, ranging from 1.2 to 15.0 per cent of GDP, which is not necessarily a feasible fiscal correction without debt relief.[b] Moreover, of the 14 countries that the IMF and World Bank classify as being at high risk of incurring debt distress, 9 are small States.[c] There is apparently a special degree of vulnerability in these economies that existing international mechanisms have not adequately addressed.

Among the inherent vulnerabilities of small States are a greater frequency (and magnitude) of natural disasters, limited capacity to respond to and recover from these disasters, susceptibility to terms-of-trade shocks, and climate change.

a The category of small States is that of the Commonwealth Secretariat, which defines them as sovereign countries with a population of 1.5 million people or fewer, plus 5 additional countries that have somewhat larger populations but share similar characteristics. Altogether, the grouping includes 36 countries (see http://thecommonwealth.org/our-work/small-states#sthash.zw1XEFYn.dpuf).
b International Monetary Fund, "Macroeconomic issues in small States and implications for Fund engagement", 20 February 2013, p. 25.
c As at 1 May 2014; joint IMF and World Bank list from http://www.imf.org/external/Pubs/ft/dsa/DSAlist.pdf.

---

6 For the complete list of non-Paris Club creditors, see International Monetary Fund, December 2013, pp. 38–39, op. cit.

d Commonwealth Secretariat, "A time to act: addressing Commonwealth small States financing and debt challenges", background paper for the High-Level Advocacy Mission, Washington, D.C., 6–7 October 2013, p. 3, applying the environmental vulnerability measure of the United Nations Environment Programme and the South Pacific Applied Geoscience Commission.
e International Monetary Fund, "Macroeconomic issues in small States", op. cit.

f Presentation by Samantha Attridge, Head of International Finance and Capital Markets in the Commonwealth Secretariat, at the 1st meeting of the Preparatory Committee for the Third International Conference on Small Island Developing States, 24 February 2014, available from http://www.un.org/esa/ffd/events/SIDS_Sideevent_Debt.pdf (accessed 28 May 2014).

In terms of environmental vulnerability, it is illustrative that, out of the 31 small States of the Commonwealth, 24 are classified as vulnerable, highly vulnerable or extremely vulnerable.[d] Small States have also had lower and more volatile economic growth rates than larger developing countries in the 2000s.[e]

When natural disasters or economic shocks occur, the usual response is to undertake emergency spending for recovery, rehabilitation and reconstruction, which is typically debt-financed if not covered by overseas grant assistance. Some affected countries will have access to concessional multilateral resources, but others do not meet donor qualifications. Bilateral official development assistance for many small States has been a declining donor priority over the past 15 years. That leaves the gap to be filled by private flows—if funds are even available post-shock—and non-concessional official flows, where the fixed and relatively costly repayment terms may not be appropriate.

The alternative to new borrowing or grant assistance is to delay non-essential public expenditures—which can be only a temporary strategy—or to seek debt relief. Several small States have thus sought to restructure portions of their debt over recent years, and some have even defaulted. For example, seven Commonwealth member States have restructured their sovereign debt nine times between 2000 and 2013.[f] Some have succeeded in reducing the face value of their debt, but in several cases there was no reduction in the debt stock; maturities were simply lengthened and interest rates were lowered (see table for the differential impact of the treatments for seven countries).

In some cases, more comprehensive debt relief based on inter-creditor equity between all components of debt is required to restore debt sustainability and spur economic growth, complemented by greater access to concessional loans, including on a countercyclical basis. However, debt relief needs to be complemented by stronger efforts to address the inherent economic and environmental vulnerabilities of these economies, starting with more effective long-term strategies for diversification and development, including improved governance and debt management, good environmental stewardship, private sector development and macroeconomic stability.

Figure
Debt-to-GDP ratios of small States and other developing countries, 2013 (percentage)

Small States
Low-income countries
Lower-middle-income countries
Upper-middle-income countries
All developing countries

Source: UN/DESA, based on IMF World Economic Outlook April 2014 database.
Note: Data of small States are excluded from averages for other groupings in this figure. Total external debt data includes private non-guaranteed long-term debt.

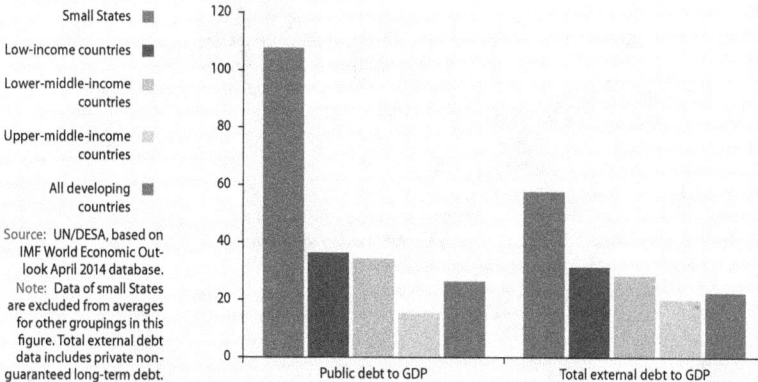

Table

Debt-to-GDP ratios before, during and after restructuring, selected small States

	Restructuring year	Three-year pre-relief average (percentage)	Restructuring year (percentage)	Three-year post-relief average (percentage)
Antigua and Barbuda	2010	90.7	90.6	95.6
Belize	2007	96.9	88.6	82.2
Dominica	2004	111.6	116.0	98.2
Grenada	2005	111.7	110.3	103.7
Jamaica	2010	127.5	143.0	141.7
Seychelles	2010	138.0	82.5	71.2
Saint Kitts and Nevis	2012	155.6	144.9	n.a.

Source: Commonwealth Secretariat, "A time to act: addressing Commonwealth small States financing and debt challenges", background paper for the High-Level Advocacy Mission, Washington, D.C., 6–7 October 2013, p. 3.

Figure 1

External debt of developing countries, 2000–2013 (*percentage of GDP*)

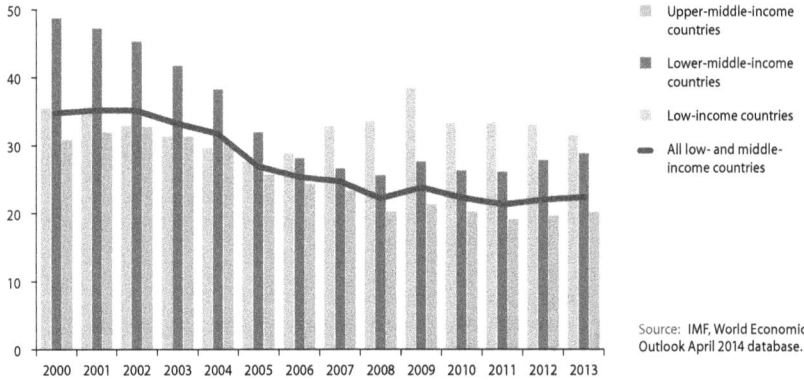

- Upper-middle-income countries
- Lower-middle-income countries
- Low-income countries
- All low- and middle-income countries

Source: IMF, World Economic Outlook April 2014 database.

...the growing share of short-term debt...

While a resumed decline in the debt ratios is warranted for a number of countries as conditions permit, one feature of the external debt that bears monitoring is the growing proportion of short-term debt in the external debt stock (figure 2). It has been growing and is significant in lower- and upper-middle-income countries. The impact may be seen in the rising ratios of external debt servicing to exports (figure 3). While the recent ratios remain below the levels of the early years of the millennium, interest rates are far below what they were then. As exports are rising, the rise in debt servicing increasingly reflects the higher principal repayments required each year. This reflects, in part, the bunched repayment of loans that Governments took out in the depths of the crisis, and also the shortening average duration of credits taken by private and/or official borrowers. While the ratios of debt servicing to exports are still mostly within acceptable levels, there is a growing risk of debt vulnerability in the short-term debt that requires effective management.

Figure 2
Share of short-term debt in external debt of developing countries, 2000–2013
(*percentage*)

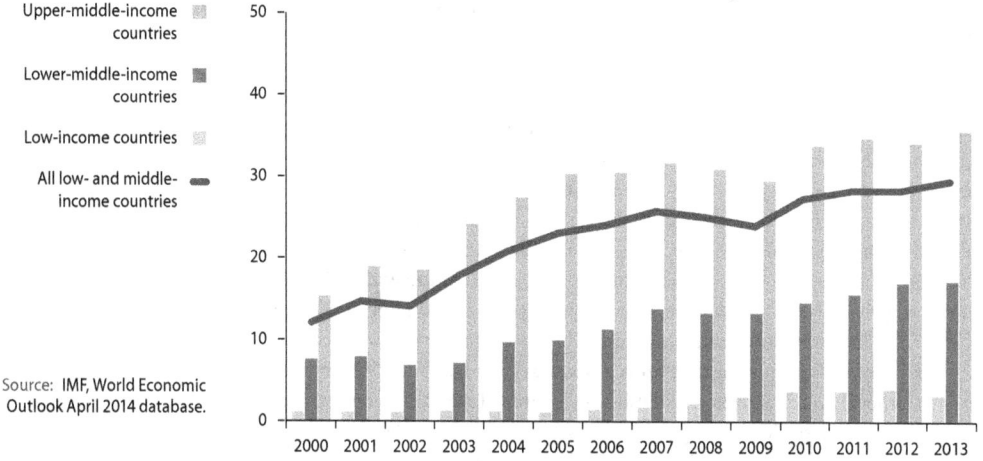

Upper-middle-income countries
Lower-middle-income countries
Low-income countries
All low- and middle-income countries

Source: IMF, World Economic Outlook April 2014 database.

Figure 3
External debt service of developing countries, 2000–2013 (*percentage of exports*)

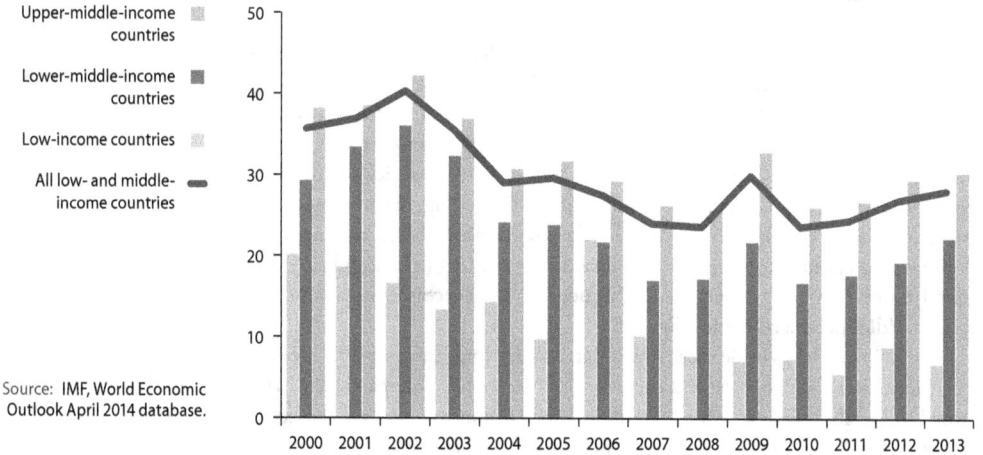

Upper-middle-income countries
Lower-middle-income countries
Low-income countries
All low- and middle-income countries

Source: IMF, World Economic Outlook April 2014 database.

In addition, an increasing number of Governments, including those of low-income countries, are issuing medium-term bonds (usually with a maturity of 5–10 years) in international capital markets. There is considerable diversity in the economic conditions of countries accessing international capital markets and thus increased vulnerability for some countries, especially those countries whose Governments have heretofore largely relied on official creditors. For example, apart from South Africa, no other sub-Saharan country floated a bond issue internationally in 2010. Three did in 2011 and 2012, raising a total of about $2 billion in each year. Another six countries did in 2013, raising almost $7 billion.[7] In the current international financial environment of unusually low interest rates, investors have sought higher yields and accepted higher risk. The present international environment, however, is no guarantee that these conditions will remain.

A traditional vulnerability for all countries borrowing in foreign currency is the potential fiscal impact of national currency depreciation, which raises the local currency cost of meeting debt-servicing obligations. This is sometimes referred to as "original sin".[8] In addition, debtors have to be concerned about maturing debt, which is usually rolled over into new credits. The higher the proportion of short-term debt, the more new debt issuance is required each year (and thus the greater the susceptibility to rising interest rates in international markets in the future). Also, the full face value of "plain vanilla" bonds[9] needs to be repaid or rolled over on their maturity date. In economically calm times, this is routine; however, creditors may hesitate to buy new bonds or extend new bank loans to official or private borrowers during a period of international financial upheaval, or if there is increased uncertainty about the prospects of the borrower country.

...and foreign-exchange rate vulnerabilities

If a debtor Government thus finds it necessary to repay a significant part of its debt rather than roll it over, it will most likely draw down its foreign-exchange reserves, if it has a sufficient supply. But it also has to either replace the reduced foreign debt with domestic public debt—and in the process possibly reduce the supply of credit to the private sector, thereby reducing private expenditure—or it contracts public expenditure. If the Government cannot repay the maturing debt, it must either borrow from a public provider, including the IMF, or default. Each scenario is economically disruptive and would be best avoided, underlining the imperative of careful advance planning in debt management.

However, while fear of any of these scenarios has underlain the push to austerity policies in recent years, austerity can also have adverse consequences, in terms not only of higher unemployment, but also of reduced tax revenues and added social safety net expenditures (where policy priorities permit). Indeed, one may see that all groups of countries increased their fiscal deficits in 2013 (figure 4), thereby requiring increased government borrowing, responding to the weaker economic growth in that year. By the same token, the current account of developing countries slipped further into deficit in 2013 (meaning larger net capital inflows), mainly reflecting the reduced current-account surplus of the upper-middle-income countries (figure 5).

Anticipating downside scenarios is particularly important for low-income countries (LICs), which have less capacity to absorb and manage shocks. The annual Vulnerability Exercise for LICs of the IMF examines changes in the external environment across countries and time in order to identify systemic vulnerabilities and assess country-specific risks.[10] The 2013 publication notes that "core"

---

7 International Monetary Fund, *Global Financial Stability Report*, April 2014, table 5.
8 The term originated from the work of Barry Eichengreen, Ricardo Hausmann and Ugo Panizza in a series of papers focused on Latin America. See, for example, "Original sin: the pain, the mystery, and the road to redemption", November 2002, available from http://www.financialpolicy.org/financedev/hausmann2002.pdf.
9 A plain vanilla bond is one with no unusual features, paying a fixed rate of interest and redeemable in full upon maturity.
10 International Monetary Fund, "2013 low-income countries global risks and vulnerability report", IMF Policy Paper, September 2013, available from http://www.imf.org/

LICs have demonstrated significant resilience over the course of the global crisis,[11] reflecting relatively stronger macroeconomic fundamentals. Also, the composition of public spending has been broadly supportive of inclusive growth.

Figure 4

Fiscal balances of low- and middle-income countries, 2005–2013
(*percentage of GDP*)

Upper-middle-income countries

Lower-middle-income countries

Low-income countries

All low- and middle-income countries

Source: IMF, World Economic Outlook April 2014 database.

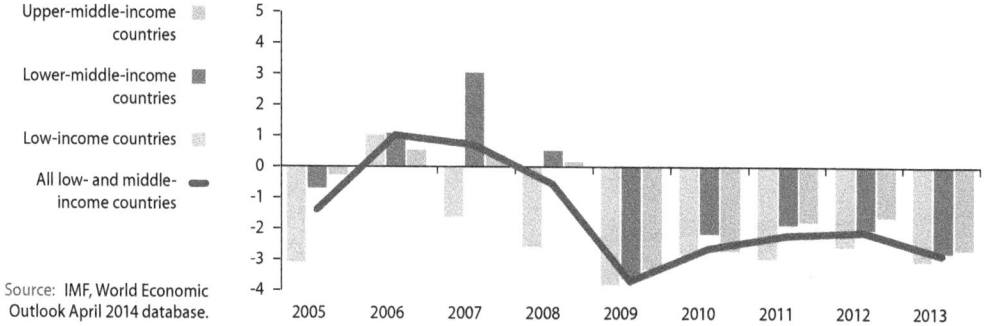

Figure 5

Current-account balances of developing countries, 2005–2013
(*percentage of GDP*)

Upper-middle-income countries

Lower-middle-income countries

Low-income countries

All low- and middle-income countries

Source: IMF, World Economic Outlook April 2014 database.

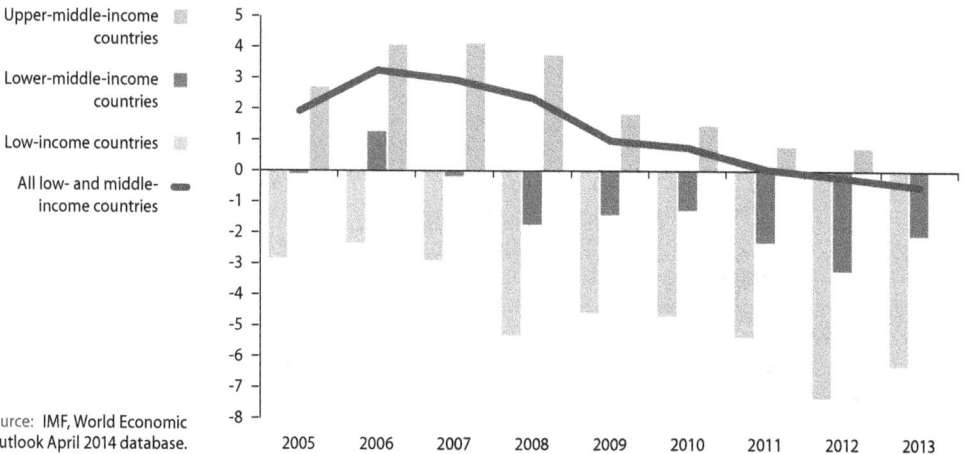

Nevertheless, since the 2008 global financial and economic crisis, there has been less room for fiscal manoeuvring; this has increased exposure of LICs to global shocks, particularly for oil exporters and small States, although core LICs have maintained some room for manoeuvre. The near-term risk of a shock-

external/np/pp/eng/2013/090613.pdf.

11 Core low-income countries (LICs) refers to a large and diverse group of LICs that do not share a specific characteristic of vulnerability related to small size, fragility or fuel export dependency.

induced recession across LICs as a group remains elevated, although moderately lower than at end-2012. Vulnerabilities are concentrated in small and fragile States and oil exporters; the number of core LICs with significant vulnerabilities has steadily declined.[12]

Multilateral and bilateral assistance for countries that are highly vulnerable and have limited financing options is crucial, particularly for small and fragile States. Country circumstances should determine the balance and timing between adjustment policies, standstills, external financing and debt restructuring, when needed. To maximize the benefits of sovereign borrowing, countries need appropriate countercyclical macroeconomic policies, effective debt management and regulatory practices in accordance with the country's specific circumstances. The degree of capital-account openness should be determined by a country's capacity to manage risk.

Frameworks to evaluate debt sustainability

The joint World Bank-IMF Debt Sustainability Framework (DSF) was introduced in April 2005 to help guide low-income countries and their donors in mobilizing more financing for development needs, while reducing the chances of an excessive build-up of debt. The 2012 review of the DSF produced some additions to the framework, including strengthening the analysis of total public debt and fiscal vulnerabilities.[13] In addition, in October 2013, the discount rates used by the Bank and the Fund to calculate the present value of the repayment obligations of the external debt of low-income countries in debt sustainability analyses was set at a uniform rate of 5 per cent.[14] It will remain unchanged until the completion of the next review of the DSF, set for 2015.[15]

The strength of a country's policies, assessed according to the World Bank's Country Policy and Institutional Assessment (CPIA), plays an important role in setting indicative limits to a country's sustainable debt. Indicative thresholds classify countries as being at low, moderate or high risk, or in debt distress. Presently, a review of the policy on debt limits is under way at the IMF, with a view to ensuring that it continues to strike the right balance between safeguarding debt sustainability and ensuring adequate financing for development needs.

Many factors come into play, which are not included in the CPIA. There has been criticism of the DSF reliance on the quality of borrower countries' policies and institutions as the main proxy to measure countries' capacities to carry debt.[16] Although policies and institutions are crucial in the long run, the capacity

Assessment of a country's policies should be strengthened...

---

12 International Monetary Fund, "2013 low-income countries", op. cit.

13 "The joint World Bank–IMF Debt Sustainability Framework for low-income countries", Fact sheet, 18 March 2014, available from http://www.imf.org/external/np/exr/facts/jdsf.htm.

14 See http://www.imf.org/external/np/pdr/conc/calculator/.

15 It is recognized that harmonization is needed between the Debt Sustainability Framework and the Development Assistance Committee's methodology for calculating discount rates for the purpose of qualifying official loans as official development to properly account for concessional flows and for the assessment of debt sustainability.

16 See for example, Machiko Nissanke, "Managing sovereign debt for productive investment and development in Africa: a critical appraisal of the joint Fund-Bank Debt Sustainability Framework and its implications for sovereign debt management", paper commissioned by the African Development Bank, August 2013.

to repay debt in the short run is determined mainly by existing public debt burdens, fiscal and export revenues, and the level of international reserves. To reflect this, one suggestion is to replace the CPIA with indices related to management, to better assess the capacity of the authorities to manage public resources. Moreover, the CPIA comprises subjective scores assigned by World Bank staff to a number of variables, only some of which are under countries' control while others are a reflection of their stage of development. Factors that might influence the setting of debt thresholds besides the CPIA should be reconsidered; the United Nations Economic Vulnerability Index (EVI) and the Human Assets Index (HAI) could be considered for introducing a consideration of structural vulnerability into the assessment.

Major economic shocks—such as devaluation, increased cost of capital and loss of growth and exports—are part of the stress tests performed in assessing debt sustainability, but structural economic vulnerabilities that increase debt vulnerability were not incorporated into the original CPIA framework. A borrower country may have macroeconomic policies considered to be sound, but it may still be negatively affected by external events beyond its control that are not captured in the DSF scenarios. Examples include environmental or natural shocks, which encompass natural disasters (earthquakes, volcanic eruptions) and the more frequent climatic shocks (typhoons, hurricanes, droughts, floods, etc.). Such factors may be analysed using customized scenarios within the DSF, to simulate, for example, new natural resources coming online or vulnerability to climate change.[17]

A more useful, albeit perhaps more challenging, approach would be to introduce an asset liability management framework. This balance-sheet approach would consider matching a portfolio of assets and liabilities, including their maturity structure and currency composition, in order to assess debt sustainability. It would allow a better understanding of the linkages between internal and external debt and the value of debt management strategies, including a full inclusion of contingent liabilities and private debt.

Besides the DSF, the IMF also carries out a Debt Sustainability Analysis for Market Access Countries (MAC). In this framework, public debt can be regarded as sustainable when the primary fiscal balance needed to at least stabilize debt under both the baseline and realistic shock scenarios is economically and politically feasible, such that the level of debt is consistent with an acceptably low rollover risk and with preserving potential growth at a satisfactory level.[18]

...as should debt sustainability and market access

In contrast to the DSF, this framework does not include debt ratio thresholds; rather, it traces the debt ratios over time under different scenarios. One of the underlying reasons for this is that benchmarking is very uncertain and sensitive, given the financial market exposure of MACs and the sensitivity of their risk premium to analysts' announcements. Moreover, estimating robust thresholds

---

17 See World Bank and International Monetary Fund, "Staff guidance note on the application of the joint Bank-Fund Debt Sustainability Framework for low-income countries", 23 October 2013, available from http://documents.worldbank.org/curated/en/2013/10/18496135/staff-guidance-note-application-joint-bank-fund-debt-sustainability-framework-low-income-countries.

18 International Monetary Fund, "Staff guidance note for public debt sustainability analysis in market-access countries", IMF Policy Paper, 9 May 2013, available from http://www.imf.org/external/np/pp/eng/2013/050913.pdf.

for sustainable levels of public debt in MACs has proven elusive in previous empirical studies. In its recent paper to the IMF Board, IMF staff agrees that in hindsight, assessments of debt sustainability and market access may have been too sanguine.[19] Following the new guidance for the IMF Debt Sustainability Analysis for MACs, there is scope for increasing the rigor of debt sustainability and market access assessments, including: having more systematic assessments and greater transparency in risk reporting; drawing on alternative stress-test scenarios; and giving greater attention to debt levels and risks to funding sources and market access. Besides the choice of analytical framework, problems in assessing debt sustainability occur because of the continued difficulties with timely reporting of external debt and contingent liabilities and the reconciliation of debtor and creditor records.[20]

Enhancing approaches to debt restructuring

Currently, there is no institution that serves the function of an international bankruptcy court for sovereign debt restructuring to provide timely, predictable and impartial solutions to debt problems. This absence has increased the cost of sovereign debt restructuring for the debtor and the creditor, and in the case of systemically important countries, has costs for global financial stability as well. Although sovereign debt restructurings do take place, these are often "too little, too late".[21] In practice, solvency problems are frequently dealt with like liquidity problems, thereby often requiring multiple restructurings. Prior to the HIPC Initiative, serial rescheduling was a common feature in LICs—as was the case in middle-income countries—that resulted in delayed solutions to the problem of debt overhang. A more timely debt stock reduction would not have necessitated the scale of resources required for the much-delayed HIPC Initiative, and would have returned countries to a higher growth trajectory more quickly. Going forward, a timely solution in cases of debt distress will ultimately reduce costs for all stakeholders.

Sovereign debt restructuring is often costly and time-consuming…

The Paris Club has been an important ad hoc mechanism for restructuring debt obligations to bilateral official creditors. However, looking forward, it is important to bear a few issues in mind. First, not all creditor Governments are members of the Paris Club. In recent years, financing flows emanating from South-South cooperation have increased. The Paris Club also excludes consideration of debts owed to multilateral institutions, commercial banks and other private creditors. Over time, multilateral creditors have informally been granted preferred creditor status. Paris Club agreements contained a provision under which the debtor would seek comparable treatment from other creditors. The implementation of the comparability of treatment principle faced many difficulties, as Paris Club agreements have no binding legal foundation. The debtor thus

19 See International Monetary Fund, "Sovereign debt restructuring: recent developments and implications for the Fund's legal and policy framework", April 2013.

20 Despite efforts in the 1980s to reconcile external debt statistics by the International Monetary Fund, the Organization for Economic Cooperation and Development, World Bank and Bank for International Settlements based on a "core" definition of external debt, these statistics are not strictly comparable and gaps remain in coverage and timeliness.

21 International Monetary Fund, "Sovereign debt restructuring", op. cit.

has no formal legal instrument through which to seek comparable treatment from other creditors. Moral suasion has worked in some cases, but in others it has led to litigation against the debtor. And now with the increase in private capital flows to developing countries, the importance and relevance of the Paris Club has been reduced.

Bond debt and bank debt now have a significant share in the composition of overall developing-country debt and pose challenges for timely and adequate resolution of debt problems with issues in creditor coordination and the threat of litigation by hold-out creditors. Despite changes in contractual terms to facilitate the so-called voluntary market-based restructuring process for sovereign bonds through the introduction of Collective Action Clauses, and although voluntary principles for a code of conduct have been identified, challenges still remain regarding how to return a country that is in debt distress to a sustainable fiscal track, how to resuscitate its growth, and how to balance the risks that debt restructuring poses to the banking system. Often, not all creditors participate in a restructuring, leading to either costly settlements or expensive litigation against the sovereign debtor by hold-out creditors. In the light of lengthy litigation against Argentina in the federal courts of the United States,[22] there is a growing view that further improvements in contractual terms are needed both to bind hold-out creditors and to strengthen clauses in bond contracts to aggregate voting on restructuring by owners of bonds of different series. Restructuring of bank debt, which is typically managed through an informal advisory club of banks known as the London Club, has also often been fraught with delays and inadequate relief.

There are limits to what can be achieved through fiscal consolidation programmes that cut expenditures and/or raise new revenues, which sometimes make it necessary to undertake debt restructuring, in particular where the system is dealing with insolvency. There is a real possibility that some countries may be in no position to return to growth and stability without a debt restructuring.

The euro-area crisis, like the Latin American crisis in the 1980s, has revealed the interrelationship between sovereign and banking sectors and the danger that official sector financing can, in effect, bail out the private sector, as was recently done in Greece. Moreover, Greece's financing package with the IMF, the European Commission and the European Central Bank (ECB) did not prove sufficient to address concerns regarding debt sustainability and did not avert a spreading of the crisis beyond Greece. In reflecting on its role, the IMF is currently reviewing its lending framework in high debt situations to prevent the use of its resources to bail out the private sector and finance an exit of private

---

22 The litigation in the United States courts between Argentina and NML, a hedge fund, has implications for the future of sovereign debt restructuring. The Intergovernmental Group of 24 developing countries (G24) in its April 2014 communiqué stated that it is "closely following the litigation in United States courts between NML and Argentina and believe it has systemic relevance and potentially profound implications for all countries. Any resolution that incentivizes predatory hold-out behaviour would, in its view, undermine the basic architecture for sovereign lending and debt resolution. Given the limited progress towards a comprehensive sovereign debt workout mechanism, emerging market developing countries may have to take leadership in facilitating dialogue." (para. 6, available from http://173.254.126.101/~gtwofouo/wp-content/uploads/2014/03/G-24-Communique-Final-ENG-2.pdf).

capital. The IMF is thus seeking to strike a carefully thought-out balance between financing and adjustment.[23]

The international community has called for an examination of enhanced approaches to sovereign debt restructuring in the Monterrey Consensus and the Doha Declaration, and reiterated the request in outcome documents of major United Nations conferences and annual General Assembly resolutions. Presently, discussions on improving the architecture for sovereign debt restructuring are being debated in various forums, including in the United Nations system. The Financing for Development Office of the United Nations Department of Economic and Social Affairs organized a series of expert group meetings involving official sector and private sector experts to develop an understanding of the key issues to be resolved in sovereign debt restructuring to rally around options going forward.[24] An expert group of the United Nations Conference on Trade and Development (UNCTAD) released the Principles on Responsible Sovereign Lending and Borrowing in 2012 and, in 2013, began a project to identify and formulate a body of principles and rules on which a sovereign debt workout mechanism should be built.[25] The IMF has undertaken a comprehensive review of some key instruments, and is undertaking further consideration of its lending policy in high debt situations.[26]

...and in need of improved architecture

---

23 See International Monetary Fund, "Sovereign debt restructuring" op. cit.; and Benu Schneider, "Sovereign debt restructuring: the road ahead" in *Life After Debt: The Origins and Resolutions of Debt Crisis*, Joseph E. Stiglitz and Daniel Heymann, eds., New York: Palgrave Macmillan.

24 See www.un.org/ffd for reports of the expert group meetings and for identification of problems and options going forward.

25 United Nations Conference on Trade and Development, "Draft principles on promoting responsible sovereign lending and borrowing", available from http://unctad.org/en/Docs/gdsddf2011misc1_en.pdf.

26 "Communiqué of the Twenty-Ninth Meeting of the International Monetary and Financial Committee (IMFC)", IMF press release No. 14/169, 12 April 2014, available from http://www.imf.org/external/np/cm/2014/041214.htm.

Policy recommendations

The task ahead for the international community remains to help developing countries prevent the build-up of unsustainable debts and deal appropriately with high debt burdens where they arise, which is to say, to give priority to debt crisis prevention and management policies. Given the interrelationships between sovereign debt, the macroeconomic situation and financial sector weakness, attention to complementary policy is warranted in strengthening the financial sector, its regulatory frameworks, and macroeconomic policies and exchange-rate management designed to deter volatile financial flows.

- International financial institutions should continue to review and strengthen the methodology for debt sustainability analyses, taking account of the expanding range of financing options available and the diverse economic and social situations in developing countries
- The international community should assure timely and equitable debt relief for critically indebted developing countries, such as in a number of small States, on a case-by-case basis to prevent resources being diverted from the attainment of the MDGs
- Governments, international financial institutions and the private sector should consider adopting guidelines proposed by the UNCTAD expert group for responsible borrowing and lending and reach consensus on taking them forward
- Debt management practices in developing countries, including modern asset liability management, should be improved, taking account of the potential impact on contingent liabilities of macroeconomic and financial instabilities, and technical assistance for capacity-building in this area should be provided
- International financial institutions should improve the registration of debt data, its timeliness and coverage, and reconciliation between creditor and debtor reporting systems to enhance the capability to monitor debt sustainability and respond to early warning signals
- Governments should strike a social and developmental balance while implementing adjustment policies to reduce excessive debt burdens
- The international community should convoke an international working group supported by experts, international organizations, the private sector and debtors to examine options for enhancing the international architecture for sovereign debt restructuring

Access to affordable essential medicines

Increased global action in recent years has led to progress in combating both non-communicable and acute diseases. However, despite more coordination in implementing coherent national policies aligned to global agreements, essential medicines remain unaffordable and insufficiently available in developing countries. In order to enhance and expand accessibility, greater efforts by the international community, pharmaceutical companies and Governments are still needed.

Recent international commitments and developments

The world community has grown increasingly aware of the global threat and economic consequences derived from non-communicable diseases (NCDs)—such as cardiovascular diseases, cancers, chronic respiratory diseases and diabetes—which account for over 60 per cent of deaths worldwide. Of this percentage, the majority of deaths that could have been prevented occurred in developing countries.[1] It is thus important, and promising, that in May 2013, the World Health Assembly of the World Health Organization (WHO) endorsed the Global Action Plan for the Prevention and Control of Non-communicable Diseases for the period 2013–2020.[2] The plan includes a monitoring framework with nine voluntary global targets. One of the nine targets aims to reach 80 per cent availability of affordable basic technologies and essential medicines required to treat major non-communicable diseases in public and private facilities by 2025.

Member States of WHO are in the process of setting national targets that fit their national contexts. Monitoring the progress towards the new global targets will commence in 2015, with the aim of holding Governments accountable for meaningful progress in this area. As NCDs impede social and economic development and are affected by underlying social, economic, political, environmental and cultural factors, United Nations country teams were urged to accelerate the development of multisectoral joint programmes on NCDs.[3] United Nations country teams will also support Governments in developing national targets that build on the Global Plan of Action, and assist Governments in the development, implementation and monitoring of these national policies.

To further focus the fight against AIDS in the global arena, the Joint United Nations Programme on HIV/AIDS (UNAIDS) and the *Lancet* established a com-

---

1   World Health Organization, *Global Action Plan for the Prevention and Control of NCDs, 2013–2020*, Geneva, 2013.
2   Ibid.
3   United Nations Development Programme, "Addressing the social determinants of non-communicable diseases," Discussion paper, New York, October 2013.

mission on "Defeating AIDS—Advancing global health" in May 2013. The Commission will coordinate consultations within regions and with civil society, think tanks and other organizations on strategies to achieve zero new HIV infections, zero discrimination and zero AIDS-related deaths in the coming decades. It will seek to ensure that the principles and achievements of the AIDS response inform a more equitable, effective and sustainable global health agenda. The final Commission report will be published in the *Lancet* in the second half of 2014.

Availability and prices

Health facilities are lacking sufficient stock of essential medicines...

Data from continuing surveys show that essential medicines are insufficiently available in many developing countries.[4] On average, generic medicines were available in approximately 55 per cent of public sector health facilities in a sample of countries (figure 1).[5] In private sector facilities, the average availability was slightly higher, at about 66 per cent. Availability in both sectors was extremely low in a number of countries.

Figure 1

Availability of selected generic medicines in public and private health facilities in low- and lower-middle-income countries, 2007–2013 (*percentage*)

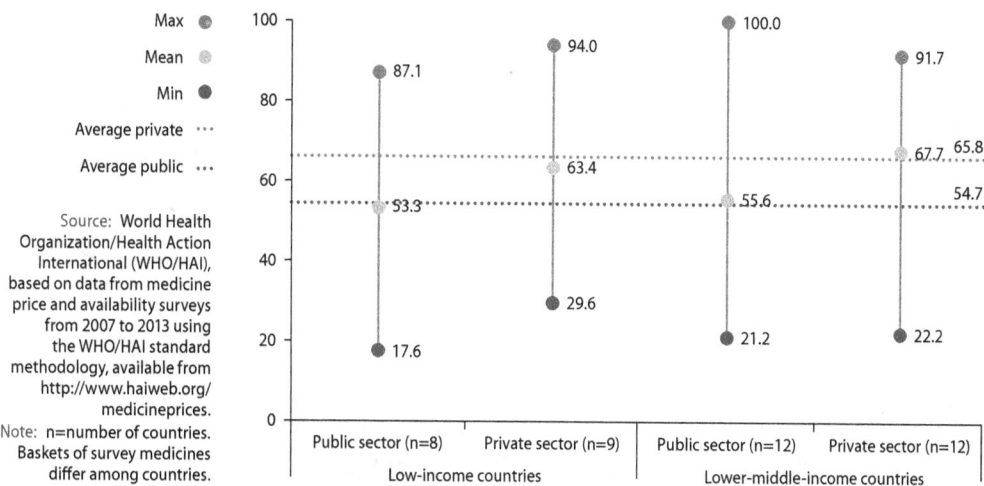

Source: World Health Organization/Health Action International (WHO/HAI), based on data from medicine price and availability surveys from 2007 to 2013 using the WHO/HAI standard methodology, available from http://www.haiweb.org/medicineprices.

Note: n=number of countries. Baskets of survey medicines differ among countries.

...and their prices remain unacceptably high

In addition to the lack of availability, patients in developing countries pay relatively high prices for the lowest-priced generic medicines. Prices in low- and lower-middle-income countries were, on average, three times higher than interna-

---

4 During the period 2007–2013, 21 surveys were conducted in low-income and lower-middle-income countries to collect medicine price and availability data, using the standardized World Health Organization (WHO)/Health Action International (HAI) methodology. See WHO/HAI, *Measuring Medicine Prices, Availability, Affordability and Price Components*, 2nd ed., available from http://www.haiweb.org/medicineprices/manual/documents.html.

5 Availability is assessed as the percentage of facilities stocking the medicine on the day of data collection.

tional reference prices (IRPs)[6] in public sector facilities and over five times higher in private sector facilities (figure 2). It must also be noted that patients in higher-income countries pay relatively more than those in lower-income ones. For example, patients procuring medicines in the public sector in low-income countries were paying on average about 2.5 times IRPs, whereas in lower-middle-income countries patients were paying 3.5 times IRPs. Similarly, prices of lowest-priced generics were 87 per cent higher, on average, in the private sector in lower-middle-income countries compared with low-income countries.[7]

Figure 2
Ratio of consumer prices to international reference prices for selected lowest-priced generic medicines in public and private health facilities in low- and lower-middle-income countries, 2007–2013

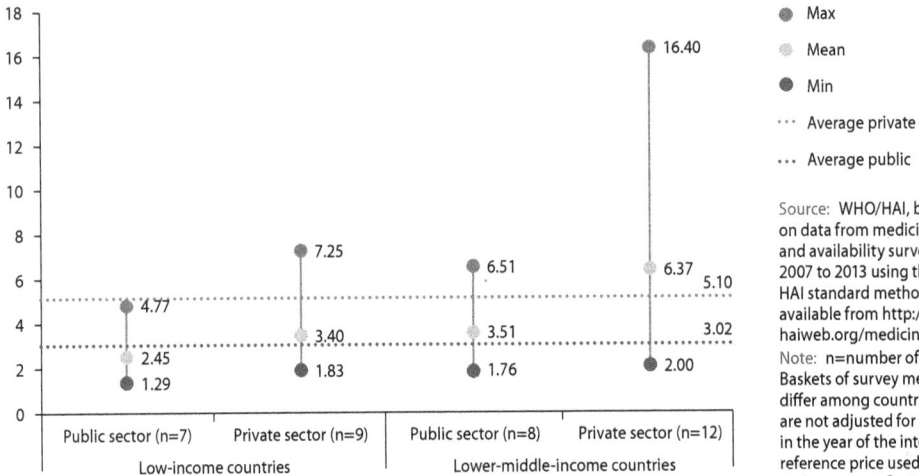

Legend:
● Max
◉ Mean
● Min
··· Average private
··· Average public

Source: WHO/HAI, based on data from medicine price and availability surveys from 2007 to 2013 using the WHO/HAI standard methodology, available from http://www.haiweb.org/medicineprices.
Note: n=number of countries. Baskets of survey medicines differ among countries. Data are not adjusted for differences in the year of the international reference price used, exchange-rate fluctuations, national inflation rates, variations in purchasing power parities, levels of development or other factors.

Although the above results indicate the average availability and prices of essential medicines in developing countries during the surveyed period, they do not show the progress over time. In order to address this, a number of countries have conducted two medicine price and availability surveys since the World Health Organization/Health Action International (WHO/HAI) methodology was published in 2003. For example, data for lowest-priced generics in the public and private sectors were compared for Indonesia (2004 and 2010), Ukraine (2007 and 2010) and the United Republic of Tanzania (2004 and 2012). In the United Republic of Tanzania, there was little change in overall availability of the lowest-priced generics, which remained poor in both sectors after eight years (figure 3). However, in the United Republic of Tanzania patient prices of these

---

6 International reference prices (IRPs) are median prices of quality multi-source medicines offered to low- and middle-income countries by not-for-profit and for-profit suppliers (where there is no supplier price, buyer or tender prices are used), available from Management Sciences for Health (MSH) International Drug Price Indicator Guide. See http://erc.msh.org/mainpage.cfm?file=1.0.htm&module=DMP&language=English.

7 Information provided by World Health Organization.

generics doubled in the public sector, and showed little variation in the private sector (figure 4). In Indonesia, the availability of generics improved in the public sector from 60 to 69 per cent, but fell in the private sector from 74 to 58 per cent. Over the six-year period, patient prices of lowest-priced generics fell 35 per cent and 40 per cent in the public and private sectors, respectively. The availability of generics remained high in Ukraine in both sectors, but patient prices for lowest-priced generics increased after 5 years.

Figure 3

Median availability of generic medicines in public and private health facilities for repeat surveys in the United Republic of Tanzania, Indonesia and Ukraine (*percentage*)

Public sector ■

Private sector ▨

Source: WHO/HAI, based on data from medicine price and availability surveys using the WHO/HAI standard methodology, available from http://www.haiweb.org/medicineprices.

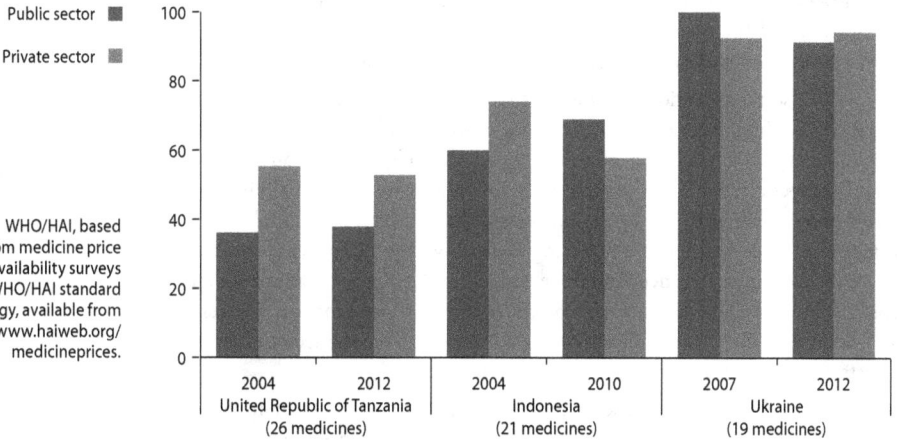

Figure 4

Ratio of consumer prices to international reference prices for lowest-priced generic medicines in public and private health facilities for repeat surveys in the United Republic of Tanzania, Indonesia and Ukraine

Public sector ■

Private sector ▨

Source: WHO/HAI, based on data from medicine price and availability surveys using the WHO/HAI standard methodology, available from http://www.haiweb.org/medicineprices. Data are not adjusted for differences in the year of the international reference price used, exchange-rate fluctuations, national inflation rates, levels of development or other factors.

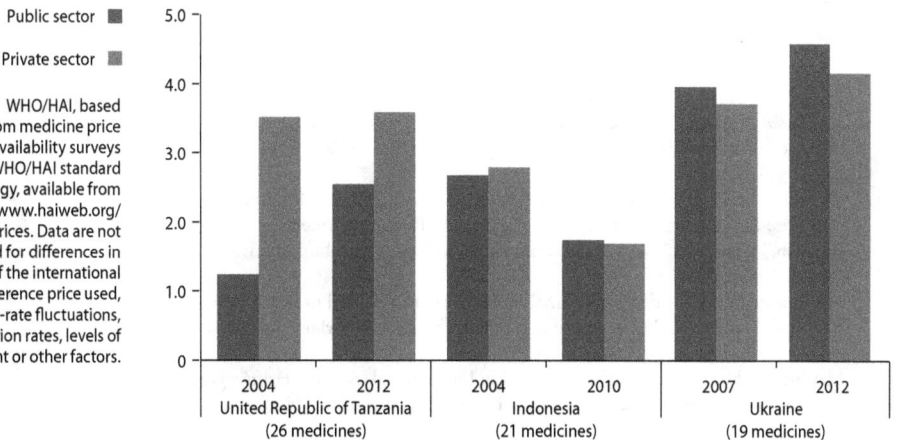

Much progress has been seen in increasing access to HIV treatment programmes, including the reduction of anti-retroviral (ARV) prices. In 2012, there were 2.3 million new infections, the lowest number since the second half of the nineties, and 9.7 million people were accessing anti-retroviral therapy.[8] However, much of the international support efforts have focused on low-income countries, leaving middle-income countries with major challenges. A new report shows that the prices paid in 20 middle-income countries for adult and paediatric formulations of ARVs vary widely.[9] Middle-income countries supported by the Global Fund to Fight AIDS, Tuberculosis and Malaria, including India and middle-income countries in Africa, pay relatively low prices for first-line and many second-line treatment regimens, comparable to those paid by low-income countries.[10] However, other countries, mainly those in Eastern Europe (Kazakhstan, the Russian Federation and, to a lesser extent, Ukraine) are paying very high prices for many ARV drugs. Middle-income countries in Latin America (Argentina and Brazil) and Asia (China and Thailand) also pay relatively high prices for a number of second-line and third-line treatments.

With some exceptions, countries that procure products from originator producers pay higher prices. These countries may take different measures to tackle this situation, for example, encouraging registration of generic products, switching to cheaper combinations of medicines, or making use of the flexibilities provided under the World Trade Organization's (WTO) Trade-related Aspects of Intellectual Property Rights (TRIPS) Agreement. Where medicines are protected by patents, voluntary licences and price negotiations can be a means of lowering costs. And where negotiations with patent holders fail, compulsory licences are an option a number of countries have used in the past (see the section below on efforts to increase access to affordable medicines).

Import tariffs on medicines may affect the patient price, but more research is needed to discern the overall impact. There is some evidence that, in general, developing countries have reduced tariffs on medicines and inputs for medicine in recent years, but that tariffs still remain high in some countries.[11] In the case of ARVs, the aforementioned survey of middle-income countries suggests that tariffs have not played a major role in most of the countries in the study. Of the countries with available information, seven did not apply tariffs on ARVs; five had dutiable tariffs of 5 per cent or lower; three did not have discernible tariffs;

Middle-income countries also need international support to access HIV treatment

8   Joint United Nations Programme on HIV/AIDS (UNAIDS), *UNAIDS Report on the Global AIDS Epidemic 2013*, available from http://www.unaids.org/en/media/unaids/contentassets/documents/epidemiology/2013/gr2013/UNAIDS_Global_Report_2013_en.pdf.

9   World Health Organization, "Increasing access to HIV treatment in middle-income countries: key data on prices, regulatory status, tariffs and the intellectual property situation," Geneva, 2014, available from http://www.who.int/phi/publications/hiv_increase_access/en/.

10 First-line drugs are the drugs of choice, or the first normally used to treat a particular condition. Second-line drugs are used to treat only those patients whose disease is resistant to the first-line drugs.

11 Matthias Helble, "More trade for better health? International trade and tariffs on health products," WTO Staff Working Paper ERSD-2012–17, Geneva: World Trade Organization, October 2012.

only two applied a tariff of 10 per cent; and one applied a tariff of 20 per cent, the highest reported.[12]

In general, countries should determine whether tariffs, taxes or producer/distributor markups are hindering access to medicines. While there has been much negative attention to the application of tariffs on medicines that has resulted in higher prices, some view these tariffs as a potentially important instrument in support of local manufacturing.[13] Where a tariff is applied carefully, as part of a targeted package of measures to support the development of an infant pharmaceutical industry, it can be an appropriate policy tool to improve overall availability of essential medicines, provided it is compatible with WTO obligations. Local manufacturing of medicines can improve public health outcomes by ensuring both the supply of quality and affordable medicines and their distribution to rural consumers (see the section below on local production).

In addition to tariffs, all low- and middle-income countries face the challenge of gaining affordable access to so-called third-line ARVs and pipeline drugs.[14] But treatment cohorts worldwide are ageing, and demand for those drugs will probably become more urgent. Third-line products are more widely under patent, including in the countries that are currently the main sources of affordable quality generics. To further the ability of middle-income countries to access ARV drugs at a price they can afford, increasing information exchange on their prices and their determinants is important. WHO already makes available databases on the price, the regulatory status and the production capacity of active ingredients for ARV medicines.[15]

Affordability

Many treatments are unaffordable

In order to improve access to medicines, treatments must not only be sufficiently available and appropriately priced, but must also be affordable to patients. Affordability of a treatment depends on a number of factors, including household income, the price of the medicine, and the regimen and duration of the treatment. Affordability is measured by using median prices and calculating the number of days that the lowest-paid unskilled government worker would need to work to buy a 30-day supply of treatment. For statistical purposes, the WHO treats anything beyond one day's wages as unaffordable. Using this indicator, many treatments have been found to be unaffordable in developing countries. For example, anticonvulsants had very low availability in the public sector in some countries, leaving patients no choice other than to purchase them in the private sector, where they were unaffordable. This was the case for carbamazepine,

---

12 World Health Organization, "Increasing access to HIV treatment in middle-income countries", op. cit.

13 See Sudip Chaudhuri, Maureen Mackintosh and Phares G. M. Mujinja, "Indian generics producers, access to essential medicines and local production in Africa: an argument with reference to Tanzania", *European Journal of Development Research*, vol. 22, No. 4, pp. 451–468.

14 Third-line drugs include drugs that are used only after the patient's disease is shown to be resistant to second-line drugs. Pipeline drugs are those that are still under development.

15 See "Global price reporting mechanism for HIV, tuberculosis and malaria", available from http://www.who.int/hiv/amds/gprm/en/.

where 4.0 to 16.1 days of wages would be needed to buy a 30-day supply in the private sector in the United Republic of Tanzania, the Democratic Republic of the Congo and Burkina Faso (table 1). A similar situation was seen for phenytoin when purchased in the private sector in Indonesia and Haiti. In Haiti, the availability of phenobarbitone oral solution was poor in both the public and the private sectors. Epilepsy can be a chronic, lifelong condition. Therefore, countries need to do more to make anticonvulsants both available and affordable.

Table 1
Availability and affordability of lowest-priced generics of three anticonvulsants

	Medicine	Availability in public sector (percentage)	Affordability in public sector (days of wages)*	Affordability in private sector (days of wages)*
United Republic of Tanzania (2012)	Carbamazepine 200mg x 150	38	1	4
Democratic Republic of the Congo (2007)	Carbamazepine 200mg x 150	6	Unable to determine due to poor availability	13
Burkina Faso (2009)	Carbamazepine 200mg x 150	0	Unable to determine due to poor availability	16.1 (originator brand)
Indonesia (2010)	Phenytoin 100mg x 90	26	0.7	1.9
Haiti (2011)	Phenytoin 100mg x 90	9	Unable to determine due to poor availability	5.3
	Phenobarbitone 15mg/5ml solution	3.7	Unable to determine due to poor availability	Unable to determine due to poor availability

Source: WHO/HAI, based on data from medicine price and availability surveys using the WHO/HAI standard methodology, available from http://www.haiweb.org/medicineprices.
* Affordability expressed in the number of days of wages needed by the lowest-paid unskilled government worker to purchase a 30-day supply of medicines using standard treatments.

Efforts to increase access to affordable medicines

As seen above, access to essential medicines continues to be a challenge in developing countries, owing to many factors that affect their prices and availability. Therefore, public and private initiatives to expand availability are important, including collaboration between pharmaceutical companies and the international community. In addition, Governments of developing countries should be proactive in making use of all means available to potentially facilitate access to more affordable essential medicines, including importation at preferential terms and domestic production wherever the capacity exists and wherever it would be more advantageous.

Public and multi-stakeholder initiatives

There are many multi-stakeholder partnerships in developing countries that have helped to improve access to medicines. For example, the International Health Partnership (IHP+) is a group of Governments, development agencies and civil society organizations committed to improving the health of people in developing countries. IHP+ tries to put international principles for effective aid and development cooperation into practice in the health sector. As at May 2013, there were

59 signatories to the IHP+ Global Compact for achieving the health Millennium Development Goals by providing adequate resources and access to medicines.

The Global Fund to Fight AIDS, Tuberculosis and Malaria (the Global Fund) was created in 2002 as an international financing institution to fight AIDS, tuberculosis and malaria through partnership, transparency, constant learning and results-based funding. The Global Fund has become the main multilateral funder in the area of global health. It channels 82 per cent of the international financing for tuberculosis, 50 per cent of the funds for malaria, and 21 per cent of the international financing against AIDS. The Global Fund's contribution to the achievement of health-related Millennium Development Goals (MDGs) has been critical. As at end-2013, programmes supported by the Global Fund had succeeded in having 6.1 million people on antiretroviral therapy for AIDS, had tested and treated 11.2 million people for tuberculosis, and had distributed 360 million insecticide-treated nets to protect against malaria.

The United States President's Emergency Plan for AIDS Relief (PEPFAR) is an initiative to help save the lives of those affected by HIV around the world, with a special focus on improving the health of women, newborns and children. As at 30 September 2013, PEPFAR was supporting antiretroviral treatment for 6.7 million patients worldwide. It has been estimated that PEPFAR managed to save about $323 million[16] from 2005 to 2008 through the use of generic ARVs.[17] By 2012, over 98 per cent of the ARVs purchased by PEPFAR were generic.[18] In March 2014, PEPFAR signed a three-year agreement with the Millennium Challenge Corporation (MCC) to support efforts to promote greater host-country responsibility and ownership in the United States global AIDS programme. PEPFAR funds will facilitate technical assistance from MCC to help advance ownership in a group of countries.

Role of patents and trade flexibilities

The characteristics of the intellectual property system in place in a developing country may affect access to medicines. In particular, the effect of the patent on access will depend on how patents are administered by Governments, how patent owners manage their rights and how Governments oversee the exercise of that right. The presence of a patent on a specific treatment creates an exclusive right on that treatment which may result in high prices. This may restrict but not necessarily prevent access. By the same token, the absence of a patent does not guarantee greater access to the medicine.[19]

---

16 All monetary amounts are expressed in United States dollars, except where otherwise indicated.
17 See United States President's Emergency Plan for AIDS Relief, "Use of generic antiretroviral drugs and cost savings in U.S. HIV treatment programs", press release, 18 July 2010, available from http://www.pepfar.gov/press/releases/2010/144808.htm.
18 Ambassador Ron Kirk, "Trade and access to medicines: working to make the two go hand in hand", 20 July 2012, Office of the United States Trade Representative, available from http://www.ustr.gov/about-us/press-office/blog/2012/july/ambassador-ron-kirk-trade-access-medicines.
19 World Health Organization, World Intellectual Property Organization and World Trade Organization, *Promoting Access to Medical Technologies and Innovation*, Geneva, 2013.

The WTO TRIPS Agreement contains a number of provisions known as public health flexibilities, which allow developing countries to protect their public health needs through the management of their intellectual property systems. These flexibilities were reaffirmed in the 2001 Doha Declaration on the TRIPS Agreement and Public Health, which stated, among other considerations, that the TRIPS Agreement does not and should not prevent WTO members from taking measures to protect public health.[20]

One of the key public health–related flexibilities available within the TRIPS Agreement is the discretion for developing-country legal authorities to determine what constitutes an invention and the criteria for awarding patent protection within their country to manufacturers. The TRIPS Agreement requires that an invention must be new, involve an inventive step, and be of industrial applicability. This leaves considerable discretion with WTO members as to how to interpret, define and apply these three criteria within their national legal systems. The precise nature of such discretion has not been tested through the WTO dispute settlement system thus far.

A recent example in India shows how interpreting the definition of an invention can increase treatment access. On 1 April 2013, the Supreme Court of India dismissed the appeal by Swiss pharmaceutical company Novartis of the decision by the Indian patent office not to grant a patent on the beta-crystalline form of imatinib mesylate, a drug used to treat chronic myeloid leukemia (CML), a type of blood cancer. More specifically, the patent on the beta-crystalline version was rejected on the grounds that it failed to show a significant increase in efficacy over the known substance (as required by section 3(d) of the Indian Patents Act[21]). The implication of this decision is that competitors of the originator company in the Indian market can continue to sell generic versions of the drug at a more affordable price. At the time of the ruling, the Novartis brand of the drug, Glivec, was selling for the equivalent of $2,600 a month in India, while the generic equivalent is available in India for just $175 a month.[22]

Access may increase by rejecting a patent…

This case was seen by some as important not only for the precedent it set globally for the application of narrow standards regarding what constitutes an invention, but also because the Supreme Court of India confirmed that India, as a WTO member, was entitled to implement its patent legislation to meet public health objectives. This, in turn, would reduce incidents of "ever-greening"[23] and ensure that only patents of the highest quality are granted in India. Some suppliers and their Governments have expressed concerns about the impact of narrow definitions of innovation in the pharmaceutical sector.

Another way of promoting the generic supply of medicines is through voluntary licensing agreements, where the patent holder allows another party the

…and by entering into voluntary licensing agreements

20 Doha Declaration on the World Trade Organization Agreement on Trade-related Aspects of Intellectual Property Rights (TRIPS) and Public Health, available from www.wto.org/english/thewto_e/minist_e/min01_e/mindecl_trips_e.htm.

21 The Patents Act 1970, available from http://ipindia.nic.in/ipr/patent/eVersion_ActRules/sections/ps3.html.

22 Patralekha Chatterjee, "India's patent case victory rattles Big Pharma", the *Lancet*, vol. 381, Issue 9874, p. 1263.

23 "Ever-greening" refers to incidents where patent holders try to retain their rights beyond the expiration of the original patent. For a discussion on ever-greening, see World Health Organization, World Intellectual Property Organization and World Trade Organization, *Promoting Access to Medical Technologies and Innovation*, op. cit., pp. 131–132.

right to use generics under certain conditions—often, but not necessarily, in exchange for payment of an agreed royalty. Many pharmaceutical companies have entered into voluntary licensing agreements for HIV treatments through the Medicines Patent Pool (MPP), created with the support of UNITAID in 2010. An agreement between the MPP and the pharmaceutical company Bristol-Myers Squibb on the ARV atazanavir covers 110 developing countries; in addition, the agreement allows the sublicensees to market their products in all countries where no patents have been granted, comprising an additional 34 countries. This should allow these countries to procure generic versions of atazanavir from generic companies that sign sublicence agreements with the MPP. In addition, the MPP recently signed an agreement on dolutegravir and is currently negotiating licences for tenofovir alafenamide fumarate and paediatric lopinavir/ritonavir.[24]

Least developed countries (LDCs) are exempt from complying with the TRIPS Agreement with respect to pharmaceutical products until 2016. They also received a renewed general extension with respect to the implementation of the TRIPS Agreement, except for non-discrimination, until 1 July 2021.[25] This additional extension provides LDCs with the necessary flexibility to facilitate the creation of a viable technological base and overcome capacity constraints by various means, including technology transfer.

Local production

The Doha Declaration on the TRIPS Agreement and Public Health reaffirmed the commitment under article 66.2 of TRIPS to promote and encourage technology transfer to LDCs, as well as the commitment of developed countries to provide incentives to their enterprises and institutions for public health–related technology transfer. The need to provide technology transfer and develop local production of medicines was also emphasized in the 2006 Political Declaration on HIV and AIDS, and reaffirmed and adopted by the United Nations General Assembly in 2011.[26]

Producing medicines locally can also increase access

This opened opportunities for South-South cooperation among Governments, as well as with the private sector. Several regional strategies, such as the African Union's Pharmaceutical Manufacturing Plan for Africa (PMPA), the East African Community Regional Pharmaceutical Manufacturing Plan of Action and the Southern African Pharmaceutical Business Plan, were mentioned in the *MDG Gap Task Force Report 2013*. More recently, it has been reported that Quality Chemicals Limited (a manufacturer considered to be operating in compliance

---

24 See United Nations, *MDG Gap Task Force Report 2013: The Global Partnership for Development—The Challenge We Face* (Sales No. E.13.I.5), for a list of recent examples of issuance of compulsory and voluntary licences and their effect on prices.

25 See "The least developed get eight years more leeway on protecting intellectual property", June 2013, available from http://www.wto.org/english/news_e/news13_e/trip_11jun13_e.htm.

26 United Nations General Assembly resolution 60/262, "Political Declaration on HIV/AIDS", available from http://data.unaids.org/pub/Report/2006/20060615_hlm_politicaldeclaration_ares60262_en.pdf; and resolution 65/277, "Political Declaration on HIV/AIDS: Intensifying our Efforts to Eliminate HIV/AIDS, available from www.un.org/en/ga/search/view_doc.asp?symbol=A/RES/65/277.

with WHO Good Manufacturing Practices,[27] and based in Luzira, Uganda),
which was created with the help of Indian generic manufacturer Cipla and the
Ugandan Government, received approval from the National Drug Authority
(NDA) to manufacture the once-a-day tenofovir-based drug duomune. This is
the first-line treatment for HIV recommended by the Ministry of Health.[28] The
company also plans to produce the fixed-dose triple combination marketed as
viraday.[29] Quality Chemicals is also listed as the producer of generic antimalarial
medicines, efavirenz (an ARV) and duovir-N tablets, a triple combination of
lamivudine, nevirapine and zidovudine.

In 2013, the PMPA Business Plan was implemented in Ghana. A study
by the Promoting Quality of Medicines project of the United States Pharma-
copeia and the Ghanaian Food and Drug Authority stressed the importance of
strengthening local production to ensure the provision of quality medicine. The
study found that the majority of ergometrine and oxytocin, two key uterotonics
imported by Ghana, were not registered and were of substandard quality.[30]

Quality of medicines

Spurious/falsely labelled/falsified/counterfeit medicines are a pressing problem
that must be addressed. There is a critical need to find legislative and policy
approaches that would reduce the spread of such products without hindering
access to good quality, safe and efficacious medicines, in particular affordable
generics. It is also important to ensure that initiatives in intellectual property
enforcement that go beyond the requirements of the TRIPS Agreement, which
are included in some free trade agreements, do not obstruct the legitimate trade
in essential medicines.[31]

Assuring the quality and safety of medicines is essential

Assuring the quality of medicines continues to pose challenges, especially
in developing countries. Two recent technological advances promise to help in
checking the authenticity of products in the market. The development of new
devices using information and communication technologies has helped regulatory officials and consumers to identify substandard and falsified medicines in
recent years, although not yet on a wide scale. For instance, a recently developed
technology operated by the company MPedigree, an innovative company from
Ghana, involves the addition of a small strip, similar to the scratch panel on

---

27 See World Health Organization Public Inspection Report, available from http://apps.
    who.int/prequal/WHOPIR/WHOPIR_QCIL25–28January2010.pdf.
28 See "Quality Chemical Industries receives manufacturing approval for Tenofovir
    based combination", press release, 20 May 2013, available from http://www.qcil.co.ug/
    index.php?option=com_k2&view=item&id=57:quality-chemical-industries-recieves-
    manufacturing-approval-for-tenofovir-based-combination.
29 See announcement on antiretrovirals, available from www.qcil.co.ug/index.
    php?option=com_k2&view=item&layout=item&id=12&Itemid=62.
30 See "Post-market quality surveillance project: maternal healthcare products (oxytocin
    and ergometrin) on the Ghanaian market", February 2013, available from http://
    www.usp.org/sites/default/files/usp_pdf/EN/PQM/ghana-mch_mqm_report_final-
    mar_27_2013_rdct.pdf.
31 See United Nations Development Programme, "Anti-counterfeit laws and public
    health", Discussion Paper, New York, July 2012; and World Health Organization,
    World Intellectual Property Organization and World Trade Organization, *Promoting
    Access to Medical Technologies and Innovation*, op. cit.

a mobile phone charge card, to the packaging of a medicine. This scratch pad reveals a unique number or code, which a consumer may then use to text a toll-free number for confirmation of the legitimacy of the package in question.[32]

The United States Food and Drug Administration (FDA) has designed a tool called the CD-3, which reportedly uses the light of alternate wavelengths to rapidly discern differences between a product that is authentic and a potentially harmful fake. According to the FDA, the device is a battery-operated, handheld, inexpensive tool that costs a fraction of the price of existing laboratory-based and field-deployable technologies.[33] While the device is not yet officially for sale to foreign regulators, the FDA has noted the feasibility of the device for use in remote areas of developing countries, and has also said that it may consider making the device available to regulators elsewhere.[34]

Policy recommendations

- Developing countries are encouraged to work with United Nations country teams to accelerate the development of multisectoral joint programmes on non-communicable diseases and develop national targets that build on the Global Plan of Action
- Developing countries are encouraged to take advantage of the flexibilities offered in the TRIPS Agreement by incorporating them into their national laws and developing multidimensional policies that foster access to essential medicines
- While efforts to increase access to antiretroviral drugs in low-income countries should continue, focus should also be given to middle-income countries where AIDS is prevalent to assure access to ARVs
- Countries should carefully implement laws and policies that address spurious/falsely labelled/falsified/counterfeit medicines in order to improve quality assurance in a manner that does not impede access to treatment

32 Will Ross, "Nigerian texters to take on the drug counterfeiters," BBC News, 10 January 2013, available from http://www.bbc.com/news/world-africa-20976277.

33 United States Department of Health and Human Services, Food and Drug Administration, "FDA Facts: FDA's counterfeit detection device CD-3", April 2013, available from http://www.fda.gov/downloads/NewsEvents/Newsroom/FactSheets/UCM349286.pdf.

34 Eric Palmer, "New FDA hand-held scanner sheds light on counterfeits", *FiercePharma*, 27 September 2012, available from http://www.fiercepharmamanufacturing.com/story/new-fda-hand-held-scanner-sheds-light-counterfeits/2012–09–27.

Access to new technologies

Developing-country access to advanced technologies, highlighted in Goal 8 of the Millennium Development Goals (MDGs), continues to grow at a fast pace. Yet despite international initiatives, gaps in access to certain key areas, such as broadband Internet, still persist between developed and developing countries. The provision of e-government services continues to spread and facilitate development efforts, but many types of services are still not provided online. Spreading the use of advanced technology for disaster risk reduction becomes more urgent as the frequency and intensity of natural disasters increases. In further positive developments, international initiatives are now in place to respond to developing countries' needs for access to technologies that address the impact of climate change.

New international commitments

The International Telecommunication Union (ITU) held its sixth World Telecommunication Development Conference (WTDC-14) from 30 March to 10 April 2014 in Dubai, United Arab Emirates, with the theme "Broadband for Sustainable Development". The Conference focused on the development priorities for information and communication technology (ICT) over the next four years, and agreed on programmes, projects and initiatives for their implementation. The Dubai Declaration and the Dubai Action Plan include agreements to do the following: foster international cooperation on telecommunication and ICT issues; create an enabling environment conducive to ICT development, which furthers the development of ICT networks and relevant applications and services; bridge the standardization gap; build human and institutional capacity, provide data and statistics, promote digital inclusion and provide concentrated assistance to countries in special need; and enhance applications to climate change adaptation and mitigation and disaster management efforts through telecommunications.

At the United Nations Framework Convention on Climate Change (UNFCCC) Climate Change Conference, held in November 2013 in Warsaw, countries decided to initiate or intensify domestic preparation for their intended national contributions towards the agreement to adopt a universal climate change agreement by 2015, to be implemented in 2020. This agreement will entail adoption and adaptation of new as well as standard technologies. The Conference decided to establish an international mechanism to provide the most vulnerable populations with better protection against loss and damage caused by extreme weather and slow-onset events, such as rising sea levels.

Developed-country Governments also provided more clarity on their plans for mobilizing finance to support developing-country actions to curb emissions and adapt to climate change, requesting developed countries to prepare biennial submissions on their updated strategies and approaches for scaling up financing between 2014 and 2020. Forty-eight of the poorest countries of the world finalized a comprehensive set of plans to deal with the inevitable impacts of climate change. Developed countries, including Austria, Belgium, Finland, France, Germany, Norway, Sweden and Switzerland, also paid or pledged over $100 million[1] to add to the Adaptation Fund, which has now started to fund national projects. Governments also completed work on the Climate Technology Centre and Network (CTCN) so that it can immediately respond to requests from developing countries for advice and assistance on the transfer of technology.

In November 2013, with the support of key partners, the World Intellectual Property Organization (WIPO) launched WIPO GREEN, an interactive marketplace that promotes innovation and diffusion of green technologies by connecting technology and service providers with those seeking innovative solutions. In addition, during 2013, there was significant expansion of WIPO Re:Search, which provides access to intellectual property for pharmaceutical compounds, technologies, know-how and data available for research and development for neglected tropical diseases, tuberculosis and malaria.

The Economic and Social Council (ECOSOC) Annual Ministerial Review in 2013 chose the theme "Science, technology and innovation (STI) and culture for sustainable development and the MDGs". It was agreed that tackling extreme poverty, inequality and environmental degradation would draw on innovations from science, technology and culture in the public and private sectors. During the ECOSOC high-level segment, WIPO, along with its partners, Cornell University and INSEAD, launched the Global Innovation Index 2013. The Index allows policymakers to analyse their innovation performance and introduce policies that strengthen their national innovation systems and enhance their capacity to develop, transfer, adapt and disseminate technologies to support sustainable development.

Trends in access to information and communication technologies

Overall access to ICT continues to increase, albeit at a slower pace

Access to ICTs continues to grow, allowing an increasing number of people to join the global information society. By the end of 2014, the total number of mobile-cellular subscriptions will reach almost 7 billion, nearly equivalent to the world population, and almost 3 billion people are now using the Internet. Mobile-cellular growth rates are slowing down, indicating that the market is approaching saturation levels. Most of the growth in mobile-cellular subscriptions is due to growth in the developing world, where penetration continues to grow twice as fast in 2014 as in developed countries, thus narrowing some of the gaps (figure 1).

In developing countries, mobile-cellular penetration will reach 90 per cent by end-2014, compared with 121 per cent in developed countries (figure 2). By end-2014, the number of mobile-cellular subscriptions in the developing world is expected to account for 78 per cent of the world's total.

---

[1] All monetary amounts are expressed in United States dollars, except where otherwise indicated.

Figure 1
Global trends in access to ICT, 2001–2014 (*penetration rates per 100 inhabitants*)

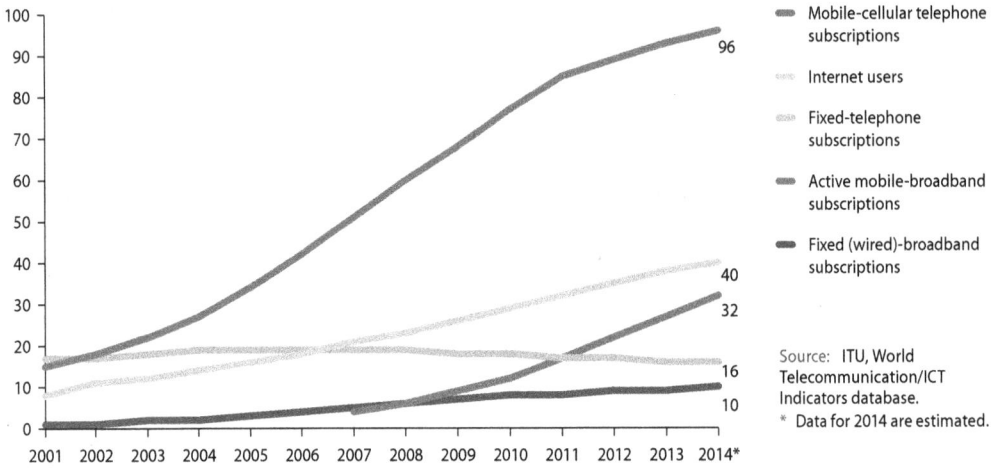

Mobile-cellular telephone subscriptions

Internet users

Fixed-telephone subscriptions

Active mobile-broadband subscriptions

Fixed (wired)-broadband subscriptions

Source: ITU, World Telecommunication/ICT Indicators database.
* Data for 2014 are estimated.

Figure 2
Mobile-cellular subscriptions per 100 inhabitants, 2001–2014

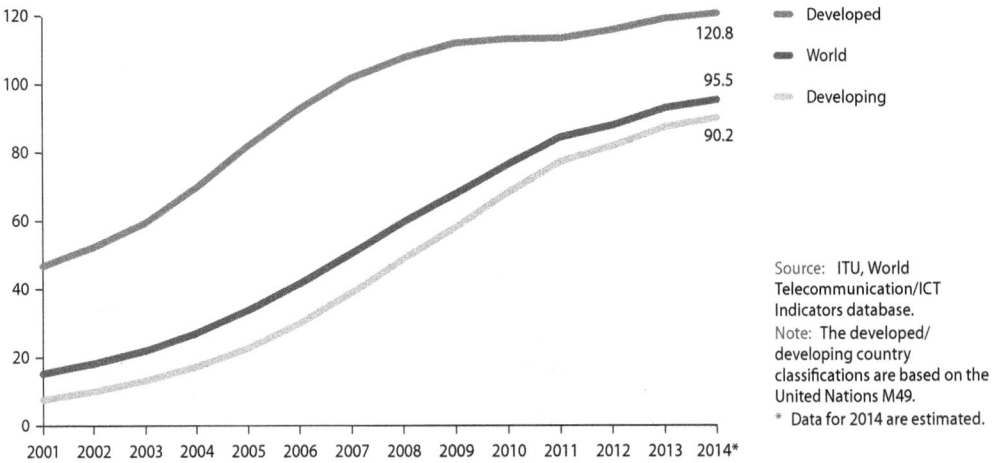

Developed

World

Developing

Source: ITU, World Telecommunication/ICT Indicators database.
Note: The developed/developing country classifications are based on the United Nations M49.
* Data for 2014 are estimated.

The penetration rate of mobile-cellular subscriptions continues to grow at a quicker pace in least developed countries (LDCs) than in the developing countries as a whole. It is expected to increase to about 55 per cent in 2014, compared with 42 per cent in 2011 (figure 3). Oceania and sub-Saharan Africa are catching up to the rest of the regions. For the first time, Western Asia joined the group of regions—the Caucasus and Central Asia, Latin America, North Africa and South-Eastern Asia—that reached over 100 subscriptions per 100 inhabitants.

Mobile telephony is growing faster in LDCs

Figure 3

Number of mobile-cellular subscriptions per 100 inhabitants, 2000, 2012 and 2013

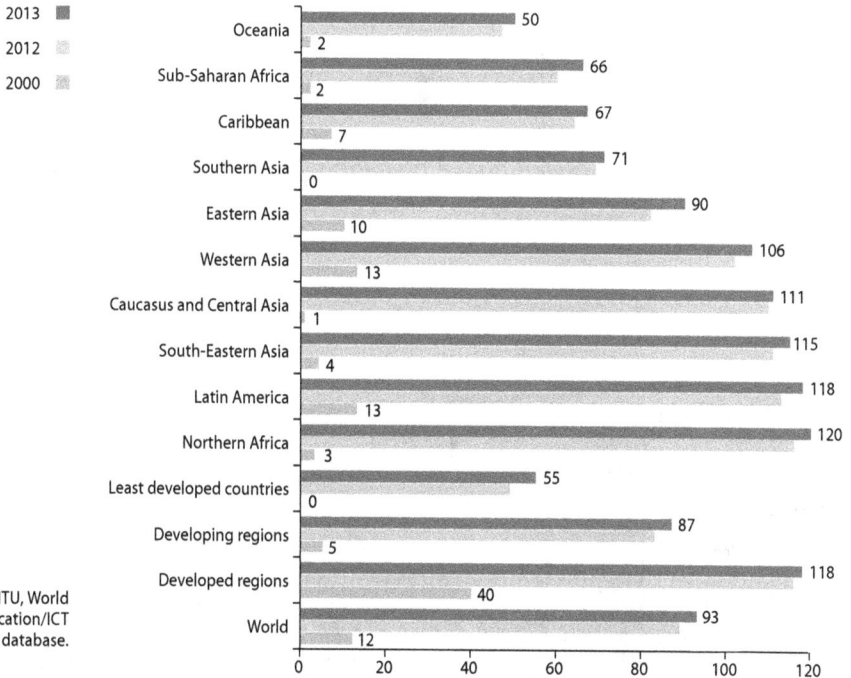

Source: ITU, World
Telecommunication/ICT
Indicators database.

As the use of mobile-cellular telephony rapidly increases, the number of fixed-telephone subscriptions per 100 inhabitants continues to fall in most developing regions, albeit at a slower pace than in previous years (figure 4). The LDCs continue to have only one fixed-telephone subscription per 100 inhabitants, while inhabitants in Oceania, Southern Asia and sub-Saharan Africa have five or fewer fixed-telephone subscriptions per 100 inhabitants.

Similar to the trend in mobile telephony, the growth of Internet usage in developing countries continues to outpace that in developed countries. However, the gaps in penetration rates for the Internet persist, with 32 per cent in developing countries versus 78 per cent in developed countries by end-2014.

Larger gaps exist in access to broadband Internet

As an increasing number of people go online, and as bandwidth-intensive applications and services require higher-speed access to the Internet, the number of fixed- and mobile-broadband subscriptions continues to grow. By the end of 2014, 711 million people in the world are expected to have fixed-broadband subscriptions—twice as many as in 2009. Total mobile-broadband penetration is expected to reach 32 per cent by the end of 2014, a fourfold increase since 2009. However, gaps in broadband penetration are much wider than in other types of ICT services. Mobile-broadband penetration is expected to reach 84 per cent in 2014 in developed countries, while it is estimated to reach only 21 per cent in developing countries (figure 5). Similarly, total fixed-broadband penetration will have reached almost 10 per cent in 2014, with 27 per cent in developed countries, compared with only 6 per cent in developing countries.

Figure 4
Number of fixed-telephone subscriptions per 100 inhabitants, 2000, 2006, 2012 and 2013

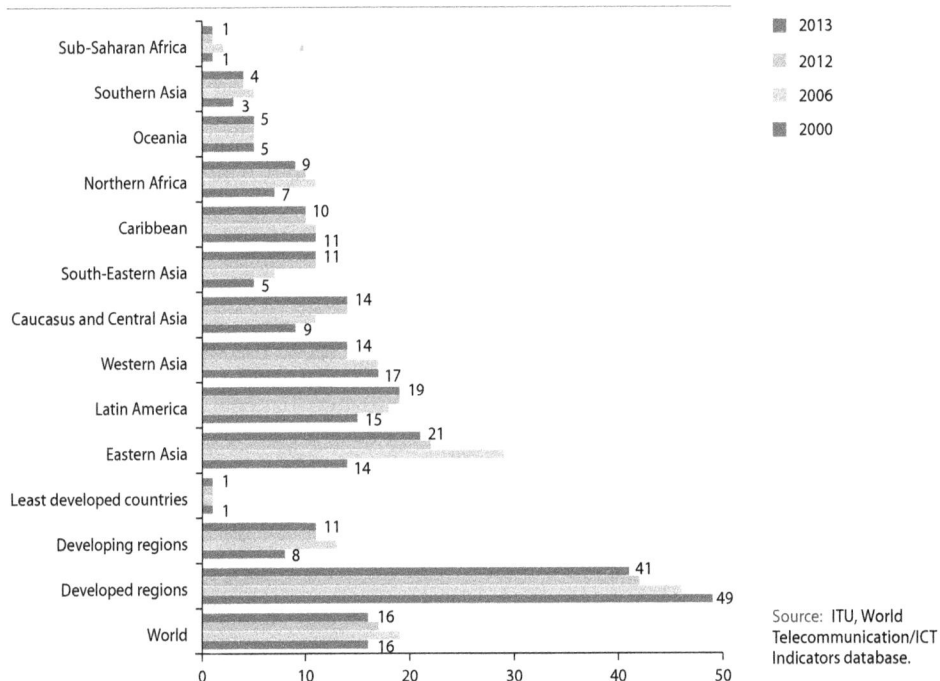

Source: ITU, World Telecommunication/ICT Indicators database.

Figure 5
Fixed (wired)-broadband and mobile-broadband subscriptions in developed and developing countries, 2009–2014 (*per 100 inhabitants*)

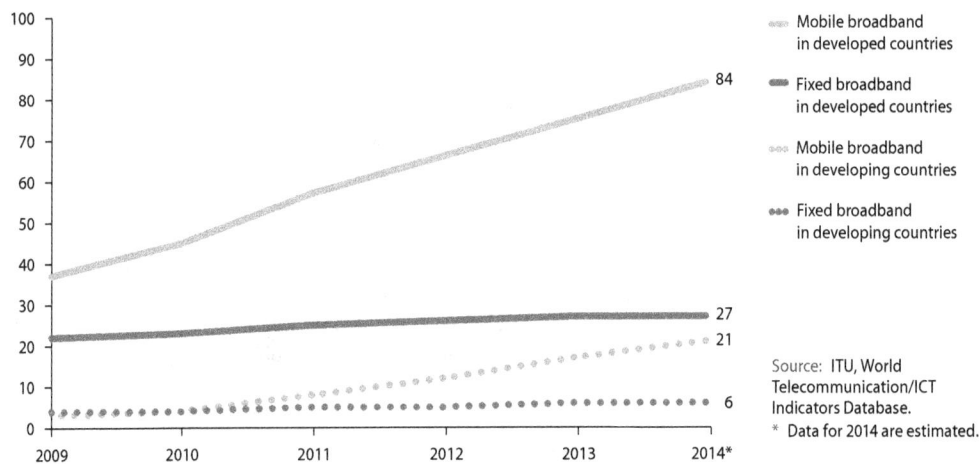

Source: ITU, World Telecommunication/ICT Indicators Database.
* Data for 2014 are estimated.

While fixed-broadband subscriptions are expected to grow at only 4.4 per cent globally in 2014, mobile-broadband continues to grow at double-digit rates, making it the fastest growing market segment in ICT services. Mobile-broadband is growing fastest in developing countries, where the 2013/2014 penetration growth rates are expected to be twice as high as in developed countries, at 26.0 per cent and 11.5 per cent, respectively. By the end of 2014, 55 per cent of all mobile-broadband subscriptions are expected to be in the developing world, compared with 20 per cent in 2008.

Access to broadband Internet is essential for economic and social development

National and international policy agendas have increasingly focused on the importance of broadband Internet for development, and the need to recognize it as a critical part of a country's infrastructure to promote social and economic development. Given the strong correlation between broadband uptake and the price and affordability of broadband services, the Broadband Commission for Digital Development identified a specific target for broadband affordability. It states that "by 2015, entry-level broadband services should be made affordable in developing countries through adequate regulation and market forces (amounting to less than 5 per cent of average monthly income)".[2]

Although in many developing countries, broadband prices still remain unaffordable to large parts of the population, the price for broadband services continues to drop. By 2012, the majority of countries, including over one third of all developing countries, had achieved the Broadband Commission's target of offering broadband services at prices below 5 per cent of gross national income (GNI) per capita. Fixed-broadband prices fell from 115.1 per cent of GNI per capita in 2008 to 22.1 per cent in 2012. The biggest drop occurred in developing countries, where fixed-broadband prices fell by 30 per cent year on year between 2009 and 2011. In developed countries, fixed-broadband prices have stabilized at about 1.7 per cent of GNI per capita (figure 6). On average, fixed-broadband prices remain by far the least affordable in Africa, where prices correspond to over 40 per cent of GNI per capita in half of the African countries included (figure 7).

Figure 6
Fixed-broadband prices, 2008–2012 (*percentage of GNI per capita*)

Developing

World

Developed

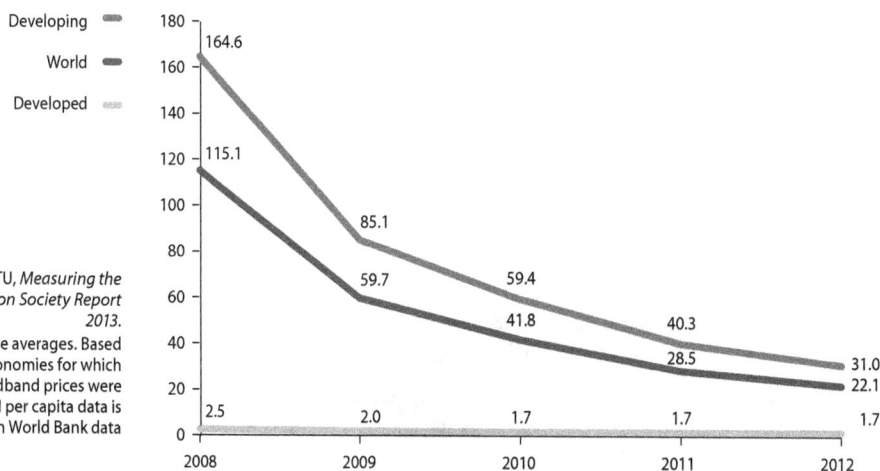

Source: ITU, *Measuring the Information Society Report 2013.*
Note: Simple averages. Based on 144 economies for which fixed-broadband prices were available; GNI per capita data is based on World Bank data

2 See http://www.broadbandcommission.org/Documents/Broadband_Targets.pdf.

Figure 7
Fixed-broadband prices by region, 2012 (*percentage of GNI per capita*)

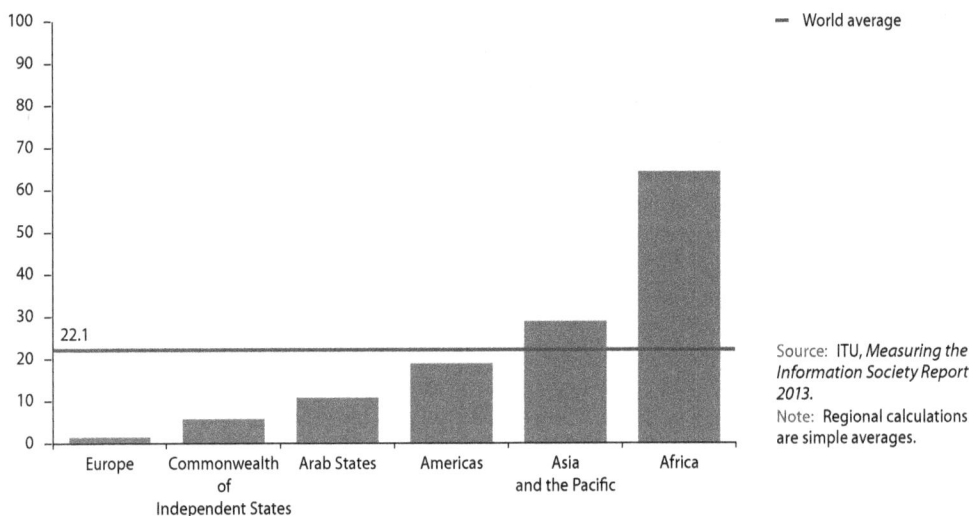

Source: ITU, *Measuring the Information Society Report 2013*.
Note: Regional calculations are simple averages.

International efforts to increase ICT access and improve monitoring

While target 8F of MDG 8 has no numerical indicators attached to it, there have been efforts to identify measurable targets, and to monitor the progress that countries are making towards becoming "information societies". These also help guide support efforts to increase access to ICTs. In particular, the Partnership on Measuring ICT for Development is a global initiative to improve the availability and quality of ICT statistics. In May 2010, the Partnership launched a new Task Group on Measuring the Targets of the World Summit on the Information Society (TG WSIS) to track progress towards achieving the 10 WSIS targets agreed at the 2003 and 2005 summit conferences on the WSIS. The WSIS targets include connecting villages, universities and schools, and ensuring that more than half of the world's population has access to ICTs by 2015.[3] To track progress in achieving these targets, the TG WSIS developed a list of 52 indicators published by the Partnership in a statistical framework document covering methodological issues, including definitions and model questions to help countries collect data on these indicators.[4]

Numerical targets help measure progress

---

3 For the list of the 10 World Summit on the Information Society (WSIS) targets, as endorsed by the WSIS Geneva Plan of Action, see http://www.itu.int/wsis/docs/geneva/official/poa.html.

4 This monitoring framework was launched at the 2011 World Summit on the Information Society (WSIS) Forum, and is available from http://www.itu.int/ITU-D/ict/partnership/wsistargets/index.html. For more information on the process of identifying these indicators and on the framework document, see http://www.itu.int/ITU-D/ict/partnership/index.html. The indicators identified to track the 10 WSIS targets include 49 indicators plus 3 indicators for a new (proposed) target 11 on information and communication technologies in businesses.

In June 2014, the Partnership published *Final WSIS Targets Review*,[5] which highlights the progress that has been made over the 10-year period since the WSIS, as well as the remaining challenges. The report shows that while extensive growth in ICT networks, services and applications and content has driven the global information society in the decade following the 2003 and 2005 summits, ICT access and use is far from equally distributed. Large parts of the world's population still have only limited ICT access, in particular in terms of Internet access, and cannot fully benefit from its potential. Besides showing mixed results for their achievement, the report also highlights the difficulties in efficiently monitoring the WSIS targets. For example, data availability is low for the majority of indicators that were identified to help track the targets. Without offering any concrete targets or indicators, the final WSIS report critically reviews each one of the 10 WSIS targets and indicators in terms of their relevance and measurability after 2015. The report highlights the need to move from measuring access to measuring use, and to focus on the quality and equality of ICT access and use. The report also suggests that the potential and importance of ICT and its role for achieving future development goals should continue to be recognized after 2015.

Another key initiative in identifying "ambitious but achievable" targets that countries are encouraged to strive for is the broadband targets set by the Broadband Commission for Digital Development, initiated by ITU and the United Nations Educational, Scientific and Cultural Organization (UNESCO) in May 2010, with the support of the United Nations Secretary-General. Through country case studies and global progress reports,[6] the Commission has made efforts to show the potential impact of broadband networks, services and applications in helping countries achieve the MDGs. In 2011, the Broadband Commission advocated four advocacy targets in the area of broadband policy, affordability and uptake, with a deadline of 2015. In 2013, the Broadband Commission identified a fifth target, namely to "ensure gender equality in broadband access by 2020".

In addition, there are presently a number of efforts to conceptualize a possible post-2015 ICT monitoring framework, and to develop new targets and indicators. Discussions focus on goals, targets and indicators and the need to link any new ICT monitoring framework to the larger development agenda, in particular the post-2015 development agenda. As part of its 2016–2019 Strategic Plan, ITU is currently discussing a number of post-2015 ICT goals and a set of measurable targets that would help monitor and track progress over the 5 years until 2020. The goals will aim for increased accessibility, greater inclusiveness, strategies for managing challenges, and expanded innovation and partnership.[7]

---

5 Partnership on Measuring ICT for Development, *Final WSIS Targets Review: Achievements, Challenges and the Way Forward*, Geneva, June 2014, available from http://www.itu.int/en/ITU-D/Statistics/Pages/publications/wsistargets2014.aspx.

6 See, for example, The Broadband Commission, "A 2010 leadership imperative: the future built on broadband", Geneva, September 2010; "Broadband: a platform for progress", Geneva, June 2011; "State of broadband 2012: achieving digital inclusion for all", Geneva, September 2012; and "The state of broadband 2013: universalizing broadband", Geneva, September 2013, all available from http://www.broadbandcommission.org/work/documents.aspx.

7 The International Telecommunication Union (ITU) Strategic Plan will be discussed at and approved by the ITU Council 2014 and the 2014 ITU Plenipotentiary Conference.

Trends in regulation

National regulatory, licensing and competition frameworks also affect access to ICT services. For example, the mobile service market has benefited from a less restrictive regulatory approach than other services, which may have allowed its rapid growth.[8] Appropriate regulation of public utilities involves a trade-off between imposing restrictions to protect customers from abusive practices and encouraging competition among suppliers, where possible. This sector has been subject to much less intervention than others, and regulation has focused on creating opportunities for markets to develop, rather than imposing requirements on what services should be delivered to which customers at what price. In the area of licensing, almost half of all countries in a recent survey have introduced global authorization regimes for some types of ICT services. One fifth of the countries opted for unified licences that allow service providers to offer new services and combinations of equipment and infrastructure more easily.[9] The main broadband markets (DSL, cable modem, fixed-wireless and mobile-broadband) supported competition in 80 to 90 per cent of countries by the end of 2013. Mobile-broadband providers, in particular, enjoyed a high level of competition at the outset, enabling operators to experience a more rapid subscription growth compared with their earlier fixed-broadband competitors.[10]

The role of e-government

Governments have increasingly used ICT and e-government approaches in public administration to attain development objectives in the areas of education, health, agriculture and poverty reduction, among others. One indicator of this expanded use is that by 2014 all 193 United Nations Member States had established online government websites for information and service delivery, compared with 173 countries in 2003 (figure 8).

Figure 8
United Nations Member States with central government websites, 2003–2014, selected years

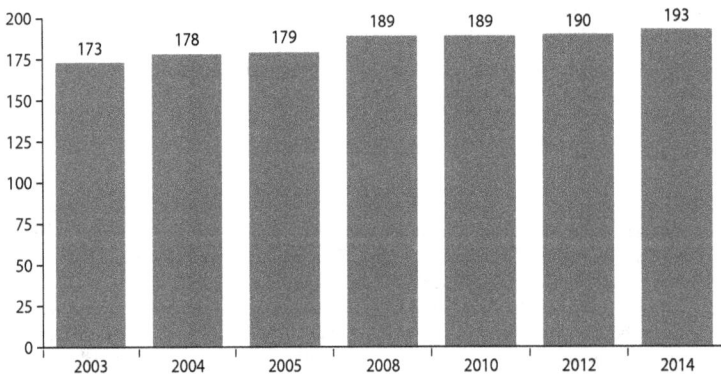

Source: *United Nations E-Government Survey 2014: E-Government for the Future We Want* (United Nations publication, Sales No. E.14. II.H.1).

----

8 International Telecommunication Union, *Trends in Telecommunication Reform: 4th Generation Regulation, Driving Digital Communications Ahead*, special ed., Geneva, 2014.

9 Ibid.

10 Ibid.

In an effort to provide seamless services, Governments have invested in strategic collaborative efforts among public organizations and departments, at both the national and local levels, integrating sectoral organizations through e-government. To this end, many Governments simplified administrative procedures, streamlined bureaucratic functions and provided greater information to promote efficiency and transparency. More than half of the Governments linked online information with second-tier local and/or regional government agencies.[11]

Nevertheless, the progress in e-government continues to be uneven among countries. While almost all of the countries in Europe and the majority in the Americas and Asia provided online information on education, health, social welfare, finance and labour in 2014, only 31 per cent of the countries in Africa provided online information on social welfare and 65 per cent on finance.[12]

Provision of financial transaction services needs to be strengthened

Although there was further progress in the provision of transactional services in 2014, the full potential of e-government in financial and service transactions, including taxation, is yet to be tapped in most countries around the world. About half of the countries provide the possibility to create a personal online account. However, there are only 73 countries where income taxes can be paid online. In 60 countries, a business could be registered online, while citizens could apply online for a birth certificate in only 44 countries.[13]

Access to know-how for disaster risk reduction

Appropriate and effective mobilization of data and information on disaster risk reduction illustrates the growth in opportunities for evidence-based and risk-sensitive approaches to development policymaking. The number of countries developing national disaster loss databases continues to grow, reflecting a recognition of the importance of detailed data in determining direct disaster losses and thus in planning how to address future losses. Further, national datasets allow a more realistic view of disaster losses in countries where global datasets have little coverage. An example of such an application can be found in the Pacific, where 15 countries have joined efforts to set up a risk transfer facility for the region. The Pacific Catastrophe Risk Assessment and Financing Initiative provides Pacific Island countries with disaster risk modelling and assessment tools.[14] It also encourages dialogue among countries on integrated financial solutions for reducing their financial vulnerability to disasters and climate change. Tools include regional historical hazard and loss databases; probabilistic hazard models for major hazards, including cyclones, earthquakes and tsunamis; and a comprehensive exposure database.

Another tool supporting the application of disaster risk reduction relates to public asset management. The first step is to create inventories of public assets, which can then be assessed for risk or to develop risk-financing solutions. Governments can then track investments in disaster risk reduction pertaining to these assets. This can align the interests of finance ministries with disaster risk reduc-

---

11 *United Nations E-Government Survey 2014: E-Government for the Future We Want* (United Nations publication, Sales No. E.14.II.H.1).
12 Ibid.
13 Ibid.
14 See http://reliefweb.int/report/world/pacific-catastrophe-risk-assessment-and-financing-initiative-pcrafi-risk-assessment.

tion objectives. For example, Mexico has an inventory database of buildings, roads and other public assets that is used for estimating exposure to risk and for designing risk transfer strategies.

Geospatial information is also an important tool in disaster risk reduction and sustainable development, as demonstrated by the practical application of satellite imagery in extracting detailed elevation data to support approaches to managing natural hazards, such as earthquakes, tsunamis and landslides. By analysing seismic intensity data, together with other geospatial information, the distribution of potential hazard areas can be predicted. Geospatial information also provides critical information to support decision makers in determining acceptable levels of risk when considering infrastructure and development projects, through the analysis of satellite imagery and the use of survey tools.

Policy recommendations

- Stakeholders should participate in technology partnership initiatives that support the transfer of technology and knowledge through information-sharing mechanisms
- Governments of developing countries, in cooperation with the private sector, should make efforts to provide more affordable broadband Internet services through an open and fair regulatory system
- Developed and developing countries should continue their efforts to connect villages, universities and schools through the Internet, and aim to provide access to ICTs to more than half of the world's population by 2015
- Considering the positive impact and potential of broadband networks, services and applications in helping countries achieve the MDGs, all countries are encouraged to provide broadband Internet to all citizens
- Governments of developing countries should accelerate their efforts to provide more information and services online in the areas that support the achievement of the MDGs
- Governments should support the development of policies which enhance the environment for innovation, while enabling faster diffusion of technologies to support sustainable development
- Countries with the expertise should continue to share information with other countries regarding more effective tools for disaster risk reduction, including asset and risk assessment

www.ingramcontent.com/pod-product-compliance
Lightning Source LLC
Chambersburg PA
CBHW052102270326
41931CB00012B/2857